1^{00}

Curriculum-Based Library Instruction

MEDICAL LIBRARY ASSOCIATION BOOKS

The Medical Library Association (MLA) features books that showcase the expertise of health sciences librarians for other librarians and professionals.

MLA Books are excellent resources for librarians in hospitals, medical research practice, and other settings. These volumes will provide health care professionals and patients with accurate information that can improve outcomes and save lives.

Each book in the series has been overseen editorially since conception by the Medical Library Association Books Panel, composed of MLA members with expertise spanning the breadth of health sciences librarianship.

Medical Library Association Books Panel

Barbara Gushrowski, chair
Lauren M. Young, AHIP, chair designate
Michel C. Atlas
Dorothy C. May
Karen McElfresh
Megan Curran Rosenbloom
Tracy Shields
Kristen L. Young, AHIP
Heidi Heilemann, AHIP, board liaison

About the Medical Library Association

Founded in 1898, MLA is a 501(c)(3) nonprofit, educational organization of 4,000 individual and institutional members in the health sciences information field that provides lifelong educational opportunities, supports a knowledge base of health information research, and works with a global network of partners to promote the importance of quality information for improved health to the health care community and the public.

Books in Series

The Medical Library Association Guide to Providing Consumer and Patient Health Information edited by Michele Spatz
Health Sciences Librarianship edited by M. Sandra Wood
Curriculum-Based Library Instruction: From Cultivating Faculty Relationships to Assessment edited by Amy Blevins and Megan Inman

Curriculum-Based Library Instruction

From Cultivating Faculty Relationships to Assessment

Edited by
Amy E. Blevins
Megan B. Inman

ROWMAN & LITTLEFIELD
Lanham • Boulder • New York • London

Published by Rowman & Littlefield
A wholly owned subsidiary of The Rowman & Littlefield Publishing Group, Inc.
4501 Forbes Boulevard, Suite 200, Lanham, Maryland 20706
www.rowman.com

16 Carlisle Street, London W1D 3BT, United Kingdom

British Library Cataloguing in Publication Information Available

Library of Congress Cataloging-in-Publication Data

Curriculum-based library instruction : from cultivating faculty relationships to
assessment / edited by Amy Blevins, Megan Inman.
    pages cm. — (Medical Library Association books)
  Includes bibliographical references and index.
  ISBN 978-1-4422-3913-5 (cloth : alk. paper) — ISBN 978-1-4422-3165-8
(pbk. : alk. paper) — ISBN 978-1-4422-3166-5 (ebook) 1. Library orientation.
2. Library orientation for medical students. 3. Information literacy—Study and
ta 4. Academic libraries—Relations with faculty and curriculum. 5. Medical
librarians. I. Blevins, Amy, 1981–editor. II. Inman, Megan, 1983– editor.
  Z711.C875 2014
  025.5'6–dc23   2014021093

Printed in the United States of America

136065

Contents

List of Figures and Tables   ix

Preface   xi

PART I   BUILDING RELATIONSHIPS AND GAINING TRUST

1   Instructional Roles for Librarians   3
Jessica Cole

2   Getting Your Foot in the Door   11
Susan Kraat

PART II   LEARNING THEORIES

3   Introduction to Learning Theories   25
Rebecca S. Graves and Shelly R. McDavid

4   Adult Learning   35
Christine Andresen and Katy Kavanagh Webb

5   Active Learning   44
Barbara A. Gushrowski

PART III   INSTRUCTIONAL TECHNIQUES

6   Introduction to Instructional Techniques   55
Rebecca S. Graves and Shelly R. McDavid

7   Audience Response Systems   61
Emily M. Johnson

8   Team-Based Learning   75
Brandi Tuttle and Adrianne Leonardelli

9   Lesson Study in the Nursing Curriculum   87
Bryan S. Vogh, Hans Kishel, and Eric Jennings

PART IV   INSTRUCTIONAL MODES AND ASSESSMENT

10   Online Instruction   95
Megan B. Inman

11   Face-to-Face Instruction   104
Michele Malloy and Sarah Cantrell

12   Blended Librarianship   112
Daniel P. Gall

13   Incorporating Self-Assessment and Peer Assessment into
Library Instructional Practice   123
Stephan J. Macaluso

PART V   SUBJECT-BASED INSTRUCTION IN HEALTH SCIENCES

14   Evidence-Based Medicine and Medical Students   139
Connie Schardt

15   Creating a Curriculum-Based Library Instruction Plan
for Medical Students   149
Amy E. Blevins

16 Librarians' Role in Evidence-Based Medicine Integration
into the Medical Curriculum 158
*Heather A. McEwen, Rienne Johnson, LuAnne M. Stockton,
Janice M. Spalding, David M. Sperling, and Lisa N. Weiss*

17 Reflections on Involvement in a Graduate
Nursing Curriculum 165
Jennifer Deberg

18 Strategies for Building an Information Skills Curriculum:
The University of Michigan Experience 171
Mark P. MacEachern and Whitney Townsend

19 What Is Biomedical Informatics? An Overview and a
Case Study 177
Carolyn Schubert

**PART VI   SUBJECT-BASED INSTRUCTION IN OTHER
                DISCIPLINES**

20 What Is Information Literacy? 189
April Cunningham and Allison Carr

21 How to Achieve Information Literacy Integration 194
Allison Carr and April Cunningham

22 A Curricular Approach to Information Literacy Instruction
in Sociology: A Case Study 205
Adam T. Beauchamp

23 Evolution of an Undergraduate Business Information
Literacy Class: A Case Study 211
Kimberly Bloedel

24 The Expanding Role of Information Literacy in the
Freshman Writing Program at Saint Louis University:
A Case Study 218
Jamie L. Emery

Index   225

About the Editors   227

List of Contributors   229

List of Figures and Tables

FIGURES

Figure 2.1.   Librarian Specialties and Activities   17
Figure 4.1.   Enrollment in Degree-Granting Institution, by
              Age: Fall 1970 to Fall 2020   36
Figure 8.1.   The TBL Process   77
Figure 8.2.   TBL Scratch Card   79
Figure 14.1. EBP Cycle   140
Figure 15.1. Finding Evidence-Based Answers to Clinical
              Questions   154
Figure 23.1. Unit 2 of Searching for Business Information   213

TABLES

Table 1.1.   Librarian Specialties and Activities   4
Table 7.1.   Hardware-Based ARS Vendors   64
Table 7.2.   Web-Based ARS Vendors   65
Table 7.3.   ARS Questions Formats Advantages and
              Disadvantages   70
Table 8.1.   Example DPT Team Application: "Finding the
              Evidence"   82
Table 8.2.   Example of TBL Class Outline for Medical
              Students: "Finding the Evidence"   83

Table 9.1.   Lesson Study Steps and Definitions   89
Table 14.1.   Sample Integrated EBM Course   146
Table 16.1.   Themes of Librarian Involvement   159
Table 16.2.   Library Instructional Sessions within the
                College of Medicine   160
Table 16.3.   Tertiary Resources Assignment   163
Table 17.1.   Review of Courses   168
Table 19.1.   Course Topics and Matching Activities   181

Preface

Instruction is a major component of the services offered by an academic library, and with the explosion of information sources and databases, quality instruction continues to become more and more important. It is often assumed that students are prepared for the rigors of higher education, when in actuality they are frequently lacking the necessary information literacy skills to become adept researchers.[1] Students are often functioning with below adequate skills and rely on their own knowledge and that of their peers when seeking library-related information.[2]

The rampant nature of technology has caused a shift in information-seeking behaviors. In addition, current trends such as evidence-based medicine and information literacy mean that one-time instructional sessions cannot provide our patrons with all of the skills they need. For this reason, many librarians are working to develop curriculum-based instruction that is semester long or consisting of many sessions throughout an academic program. In addition to teaching, librarians are also becoming embedded in the curriculums they support by serving as web-based course designers, problem-based learning facilitators, or members of curriculum committees.

Although it is fairly obvious that library instruction is important and that librarians should be equipped to provide this instruction, the majority of ALA accredited programs offer only one course on library instruction, the courses are only available as electives, and they are often only offered once a year.[3] As stated by McAdoo and supported by the fact that instructional tracks are virtually nonexistent in library schools, librarians need to gain their instructional experiences through real-life experiences, mentors, and of course, books like this one.[4]

Many books commonly discuss one-shot sessions and provide tips for getting the most out of that type of instruction. There are not as many that discuss curriculum-based instruction in a section, let alone an entire book.[5] This book will encourage readers to move past the one-shot instructional sessions by providing best practices and examples of ways that other librarians have established curriculum-based programs. It will also discuss some of the basic principles for instruction which should appeal to those who are either novices or experts in library instruction. Furthermore, this book will use case studies to explore and discuss the expanding roles of librarians in the curriculum of higher education settings.

Librarians are considered to be embedded in the curriculum or providing curriculum-based instruction when they are fulfilling roles such as but not limited to semester-long or multi-session instructor, web-based course designer, problem-based learning facilitator, and/or member of a curriculum committee. In addition to describing the roles that librarians have in supporting curriculum, this book describes how to carry out various roles with sections devoted to adult learning theory, teaching methods, developing learning objectives, and working with faculty to develop curriculum. Case studies of library sessions devoted to information literacy, evidence-based practice, and biomedical informatics are also included. In addition, the importance of context-appropriate assessment and evaluation is discussed. This book will not be limited to one mode of delivering information and will cover examples of face-to-face, distance, and blended learning initiatives.

This book is broken down into six parts. The first part focuses on the initial process of becoming involved with faculty and provides stories and tips for becoming a part of a curriculum committee or working to increase the amount of time students spend in library instruction sessions. The second part of the book concentrates on learning theories such as adult and active learning. The third part of the book focuses on instructional techniques. It includes chapters on audience response systems, team-based learning, and so on. The fourth part is based on modes of instruction and assessment, and full chapters are devoted to current trends such as online instruction and blended learning. The fifth and sixth parts of this book are introductions to evidence-based practice, information literacy, and bioinformatics and include case studies that describe in detail how to carry out subject specific curriculum-based instruction. These parts focus on health sciences and other disciplines, respectively. With this book and a little bit of determination, you will be well on your way to designing your own curriculum-based library instruction program.

NOTES

1. Gascho Rempel H, Davidson J. Providing information literacy instruction to graduate students through literature review workshops. *Issues in Science and Technology Librarianship.* 2008(53):2.

2. Gross M, Latham D. What's skill got to do with it? Information literacy skills and self views of ability among first year college students. *Journal of the American Society for Information Science and Technology.* 2012;63(3):574–583.

3. Detlefsen EG. Teaching about teaching and instruction on instruction: A challenge for health sciences library education. *J Med Libr Assoc.* Oct 2012;100(4):244–250.

4. McAdoo ML. *Fundamentals of Library Instruction.* Chicago, IL: American Library Association; 2012.

5. Detlefsen EG. 3.

I

BUILDING RELATIONSHIPS
AND GAINING TRUST

1

Instructional Roles for Librarians

Jessica Cole

The field of librarianship has been in a state of flux for several years as technological advances have impacted the more traditional library services historically offered. Physical libraries have transitioned from being quiet reading rooms into spaces with new design elements that encourage collaboration. Librarians are replacing physical collections with digital resources, turning book stacks into cafes, and unchaining themselves from reference desks. The work that librarians do is also accompanying these changes we see in building spaces and collections. Many librarians are also continuously redefining their roles to change with the times. The importance of flexibility and embracing change is the new mantra in library school. It is time to get excited about trying new things.

Librarians today often wear many different hats. Teaching librarians and those in liaison roles are getting out more; they are no longer waiting for invitations, but actively seeking opportunities to embed themselves. When it comes to information literacy or other library-related types of instruction, the content, approach, type of involvement, and various roles are constantly evolving. There are excellent opportunities to get creative, mix up approaches, and try new things. Librarians have the ability to creatively define their roles, embed themselves, and pave the way!

A review of the literature reveals several activities that have been taken on by librarians who are integrated in the curriculum. Most of the individual activities can be loosely associated with a specific category, or what we will call in this chapter a "specialty" area, as shown in table 1.1.

Table 1.1. Librarian Specialties and Activities

Specialty	Instructional Designer	Educator	Information Technologist	Liaison	Information Specialist
	Table 1.1A Focus: Instruction			*Table 1.1B Focus: Collaboration*	
Description	Creates instructional experiences through a process such as ADDIE: analysis, design, development, implementation, and evaluation.	Delivers instructional content in a face-to-face, virtual, or hybrid environment; provides ongoing group and one-on-one training; supplies feedback for improvement.	Provides expertise on various library systems and technological tools, including integrated library systems and digital collections.	Provides specialized assistance to a department, school, or program; regularly communicates between these users and the library; stays up-to-date with faculty research activities.	Evaluates, acquires, organizes, and retrieves information, and assists or trains others to efficiently access information resources and use the library.
Activities	– Conducts needs assessment – Designs learning objects and lesson plans – Evaluates impact of overall educational program	– Provides information literacy instruction in the classroom – Is embedded in a semester-long online course	– Maintains library website – Preserves digital resources – Manages link resolvers and access tools – Utilizes audience response systems	– Attends departmental meetings and events – Disseminates specialized news and information – Publicizes library services – Develops special collections – Participates in accreditation visits	– Provides reference services – Conducts literature searches – Offers tours and orientation sessions

This table is meant to help you start thinking about activities you would associate with various specialty areas that could possibly be incorporated into a new or "evolving" role. The table is broken down into two sections: table 1.1A examines these roles with an instruction focus: Instructional Designer, Educator, and Information Technologist, and table 1.1B examines roles that can be thought of as having a collaboration focus: Liaison and Information Specialist. Keep in mind that there is overlap between the categories. For example, the activity of designing learning objects, which is listed under Instructional Designer, could also be conducted by Educator as well as those in other categories. The intent is to get you thinking of all of the potential possibilities. How could some of these activities be mixed and matched for the work you are doing as a curriculum-integrated librarian or as someone aspiring to work more closely with the curriculum?

ROLES WITH AN INSTRUCTIONAL FOCUS

Instructional Designer

Instructional designers create learning experiences and materials with the end goal being student achievement of planned learning outcomes. Many teaching librarians use various instructional design models as a framework to plan programs and instruction sessions for in-person, online, and hybrid learning experiences. While several instructional design models exist, most consist of these five general phases that are referred to as the ADDIE model: (1) analysis, (2) design, (3) development, (4) implementation, and (5) evaluation.[1]

Librarians in the curriculum may or may not use a formal instructional design process, but they will likely incorporate elements of the ADDIE model, whether it is intentional or not. Examples of the activities performed by instructional designers include

- Conducting a user needs assessment (analysis)
- Designing learning objects and lesson plans (design)
- Selecting material for use that will support learning objectives (development)

- Planning instruction sessions and ways of engaging students (development)
- Teaching classes and facilitating learning activities (implementation)
- Evaluating the impact of an instruction session or program through formative and/or summative methods of assessment (evaluation)

A librarian embedded in an online course for physician assistant students at Pace University develops content for delivery through the Blackboard interface and reflects upon materials, methods, and assessment data to determine whether learning outcomes are being met; the librarian strives to continue improving the overall experience for students and plans changes for future courses.[2] The process of careful reflection over time to update materials, methods, and maximize the impact of the learning experience in this example incorporates elements of each of the five phases of instructional design.

Educator

While there is obvious overlap between instructional design and the role of the educator, it is the teacher who actually delivers the instructional content and works with the students. As librarians become more integrated with the curriculum, opportunities to teach expand. The trend away from one-shot instruction sessions by librarians is, of course, the purpose of this book and cause for excitement. In the health sciences, there is a trend to move beyond stand-alone instruction sessions, and many librarians are supporting evidence-based medicine curriculum specifically.[3] Additionally, more instruction is taking place outside of the library, with the librarian going directly to the user.[4] The topics that are most frequently taught in the health sciences are database searching, information sources, and formulation of searchable questions,[5] which are included in the following examples of educator activities:

- Teaching students how to write a searchable clinical question in a classroom setting
- Teaching how to search PubMed entirely online, with screencasts and other materials made available to students through an interface such as Desire2Learn, Moodle, or Blackboard Learn

- Providing students with feedback on assignments
- Working with individual students or small groups to recommend information sources to consult for background information

Information Technologist

An information technologist provides expertise on various library systems, tools, and technology, including automated library systems and digital collections. While this might not stand out as being prevalent in something like teaching literature searching skills to students, individual pieces of knowledge are crucial when it comes to something such as access. With the rapid advancement of technology, librarians can always be on the lookout for new emerging technologies. One example of a more recent trend is the use of audience response systems in the classroom, which will be discussed more in depth in another chapter. Knowledge of emerging technologies is helpful in the classroom setting, and especially for librarians who are embedded in online courses and working with students through course management systems. The following are examples of activities that a curriculum-integrated librarian wearing the information technologist hat might engage in:

- Maintaining the subject area of a library website or the overall library page
- Acquiring and organizing digital resources for a user group
- Managing access tools in an embedded online course
- Arranging content in a course management system
- Experimenting with new instructional technologies in face-to-face courses

COLLABORATIVE ROLES WITH FACULTY

There are many opportunities for collaboration, and in this section, we will consider activities that make up two other "specialty" areas within librarianship: Liaison and Information Specialist. A challenge with collaboration that has been noted many times is the resistance of faculty to partner with a librarian for instructional purposes. Remember that a single positive experience with faculty can cause a buzz and lead to invitations from others, resulting in deeper integration over time. Techniques for building relationships and overcoming this potential barrier will be addressed in the next section.

A special opportunity presents itself to librarians that are fortunate enough to work with programs that are brand new to an institution. Northern Arizona University welcomed its very first cohort of physician assistant (PA) students to the Phoenix Biomedical Campus in the summer of 2012. Due to the requirement of instruction in evidence-based medicine by the Accreditation Review Commission on Education for the Physician Assistant, faculty members were eager to collaborate with a librarian experienced with evidence-based practice concepts. The librarian works with students multiple times throughout the two-year program, offering specialized instruction during their courses. In addition to integrating several case-based literature searching sessions into regularly scheduled class times, faculty invited the librarian to write final exam questions and provide feedback on student projects and presentations.

The following are some examples of ways librarians can collaborate with faculty:

- Work together on a course syllabus
- Design assignments collaboratively
- Share teaching responsibilities
- Assist with grading papers and evaluating projects and presentations
- Work together on research projects

Liaison

A library liaison serves as the designated point of contact for a particular user group and communicates regularly between that group and the library. Oftentimes, a liaison is also a subject expert who provides highly specialized assistance to a department, school, or program. The group that the liaison serves might not use the library in a physical sense, but rather the librarian offers services in its work environment. There is emphasis on outreach and relationship building for liaisons; historically, the primary role has been collection development.[6]

Liaisons might participate in the following activities:

- Attending departmental meetings and events on a regular basis
- Disseminating specialized news and information of interest
- Publicizing library services
- Communicating to the library the highlights of news and research activities of a particular college or program
- Developing special collections
- Participating in accreditation visits
- Offering library instruction, tailored specifically to the needs of the department they serve
- Serving on curriculum committees

Information Specialist

Last but not least is what is at once perhaps the most obvious and important, the role of information specialist. There is overlap between all of the specialty areas of librarianship that have been listed, but at the highest level, the purpose of all of these tasks, and the purpose of curriculum-integrated instruction as well, is to ultimately connect the user with the information that he or she needs. A subject specialist would fit into this category. Oftentimes, librarians who are subject specialists are required to have a second master's degree in that field. An information specialist, whether serving at a paraprofessional level or as a subject specialist librarian, is likely to carry out and participate in these types of activities:

- Offering library tours and orientation
- Providing reference services
- Assisting library users with the catalog
- Conducting database searches and/or assisting users with formulating effective search strategies

Review the table in this chapter for brief descriptions and examples of activities from the specialty tracks mentioned earlier. Keep in mind that some activities cross over into other areas, and the specialties might be defined differently from one institution to the next. Think of each specialty as a bucket from which individual activities can be selected, and then mix and match them as you plan methods to integrate yourself into the curriculum.

CONCLUSION

Librarians who teach have the ability to embed themselves into a department or program. This is also true for librarians who currently only provide one-shot instructional sessions. While it can take time and perseverance to establish credibility and gain trust with faculty, it is possible to build on that one-shot instructional session and become increasingly integrated. It begins with a strong knowledge of the curriculum and ideas about what you can bring as a librarian, followed by relationship-building efforts. From there, roles can be creatively defined and tweaked over time as needs and interests evolve. Don't be afraid to try new things or to give up the "old" things that no longer seem to fit. Librarians should not stand by passively waiting to be asked for assistance at a point of need. Seek and act upon opportunities to become more closely integrated with curricula, with the ultimate goal of making a positive impact on the institution's educational goals.

NOTES

1. Frey B. Instructional design basics. In: Alman S, Tomer C, Lincoln ML, eds. *Designing Online Learning: A Primer for Librarians.* Santa Barbara, CA: Libraries Unlimited; 2012:1–12.

2. Kealey S. Continual evolution: The experience over three semesters of a librarian embedded in an online evidence-based medicine course for physician assistant students. *Med Ref Serv Q.* 2011;30(4):411–425.

3. Just ML. Is literature search training for medical students and residents effective? A literature review. *J Med Libr Assoc.* 2012;100(4):270–276.

4. Cooper ID, Crum JA. New activities and changing roles of health sciences librarians: A systematic review, 1990–2012. *J Med Libr Assoc.* 2013;101(4):268–277.

5. Brettle A. Evaluating information skills training in health libraries: A systematic review. *Health Info Libr J.* 2007;24 Suppl 1:18–37.

6. Shumaker D. Embedded librarians in higher education. In: *The Embedded Librarian: Innovative Strategies for Taking Knowledge Where It's Needed.* Medford, NJ: Information Today, Inc.; 2012:43–68.

2

Getting Your Foot in the Door

Susan Kraat

In the previous chapter, you were exposed to some of the roles that librarians may take on in the pursuit of developing longitudinal curriculum-based instruction. In this chapter, the focus will be on sharing tips and techniques for building relationships with faculty members to facilitate taking on the previously mentioned roles.

If information literacy is a process vital to informed citizens of the 21st century, librarians and/or faculty need to teach it to their students: either by themselves or as a team. Librarians are skilled "information professionals" who often take the lead in teaching information literacy concepts for academic and practical research and in encouraging the use of evidence-based practice(s).[1] Despite their best efforts, however, they may find it difficult to persuade some faculty colleagues of the value of ongoing information literacy or evidence-based practice instruction. On the other hand, in many colleges and universities, faculty regularly partner with librarians in providing such instruction for their students.

Before becoming a librarian, I was a buyer for a small chain of specialty stores, where I learned firsthand about "getting your foot in the door." A traveling salesman once ruefully told me the sad story of his driving through whiteout conditions to reach a store in upstate New York. When he finally arrived, the buyer refused to see him. She said, "Nobody asked you to come," a response that might be an apt title for a future autobiography. The good news is that librarians are seldom treated quite so heartlessly by faculty, but they may need to exercise persistence and patience

11

in making initial contact. In fact, promoting library instruction to faculty can be fun, especially when it is challenging. Later in this book, you will see several case studies that discuss situations when librarians and faculty truly collaborate.

GETTING READY TO COLLABORATE

Who is likely to initiate requests for such partnerships? Generally it is a librarian who contacts a faculty member, to offer information literacy instruction as an effective way to improve student research. In a recent article reviewing the literature on faculty relationships with librarians, Sue Phelps and Nicole Campbell write, "It is clear that the importance of the relationship is primarily to librarians."[2] Even if faculty and their students stand to benefit from library instruction, they may not know exactly what librarians have to offer. So how is a librarian to get started?

Information management/literacy (IM/IL) is a process that a student/user learns to navigate and utilize myriad forms of information. Library instruction offers direct assistance in IM/IL mastery and in the use of evidence-based practice for student research projects. At the same time, it is a powerful marketing tool for many library resources and services. It can take place in multiple formats, from one or more face-to-face sessions, to librarians embedded within online or traditional courses, all the way to true partnerships, such as teaching courses for credit. While all of these formats educate students to use information effectively and to think critically, they are also dependent upon positive interaction between librarians and departmental faculty. How do such relationships begin? At one time or other, you may have skimmed Terri L. Holtze's "100 Ways to Reach Your Faculty," a 2002 conference paper that impressed an enthusiastic group of academic librarians hungry for ways to get faculty to respond to their efforts. It is hard to top a paper that offers such an impressive number of ideas, many of which are still fresh and relevant today. She categorizes the 100 ways under broad categories: "Meeting Your Faculty, Building Relationships, Communicating Professionally, Positioning the Library, Knowing Your Stuff, and Collaborating with Faculty."[3] I would also add "Having a Plan."

Have a plan before you initiate contact. Familiarize yourself with your institution's library instruction program, its goals and objectives. Discuss these with your teaching librarian colleagues. If your institution does not have a plan (or even if it does), learn about what other people are doing. Does your library offer mainly single course-related face-to-face sessions? Are there any credit courses, alone or associated with a discipline? What are you prepared to bring to the table? Look at courses and syllabi. Be ready for questions and proceed with confidence.

MEETING FACULTY: SHOW THEM WHAT YOU CAN DO

Assume a positive outcome when you reach out to faculty. All it may take to get started is a faculty announcement about the availability of library instruction. In programs where there is a mandate for the inclusion of information literacy as a competency, your service will likely be promoted by administration. Once you have a commitment, virtually or in person, it is up to you to show what you can do.

In their article about librarians' teaching experiences, Heidi Julien and Jen Pecoskie speak of a "separation between librarians' and faculty members' experiences on campus; collaboration, or the need for faculty-librarian relationships to foster information literacy initiatives; and librarians as advocates, which argues that success for information literacy initiatives lies with librarians, especially in building effective relationships with teaching faculty." Time is the enemy. Writing about the "gift of time," the authors describe the faculty member as the "giver" of this valuable commodity, while the teaching librarian is the "receiver."[4] While respect for the constraints of the faculty member's responsibilities is a key element in making initial contact, the librarian need not feel inferior. In his article "Can't Get No Respect: Helping Faculty to Understand the Educational Power of Information Literacy," William Badke points out the increasing number of mandates to include IL instruction as part of curricular reform. Here the librarian as "information expert" may feel more confident knowing he or she is offering a service that engages students in a process that will help them all their lives. Nonetheless he or she acknowledges that some "faculty culture can be a hard nut to crack."[5] In that case, what are your options?

Take Advantage of Library Liaison Programs

A library liaison program provides a natural entrée. As your university's go-to person, responsible for seeing that a department's library requirements are met, you may be welcomed by faculty at a department meeting. Contact the chair to ask for a few minutes to describe a new library service or database. Being there in person often leads to a dialogue with faculty and can provide an opportunity for you to shine. Highlight what you and the library can do for the department. Ask for a realistic amount of time, and you may be surprised at the results. The first meeting of the year may work, before the semester revs up. If that is no go, keep trying. In interviews with teaching librarians from State University of New York (SUNY) New Paltz, all of whom participate in a Library Liaison program, most said they have used this approach. Be understanding about time constraints and faculty pressures, but also be persistent.

Faculty may be responsible for working with the library liaison role for their department as well. As described in the previous chapter, there is much to be gained from regular interaction with someone within a department. Liaison programs can lead to other opportunities for librarians, such as serving on a departmental search committee or helping with assessment projects.[6] If you receive no response from a faculty member, try sending a link to a tutorial, a video, or a guide you have created. Even better, offer to tailor a guide to the specific needs of the class. Use social media as well. All it takes is word of mouth among faculty to make your service popular. Confer with librarian colleagues about successes they have had. Almost all of them are happy to share good (and bad) moments. Their advice can be invaluable. Finally, remember to seek assistance from your library director or dean, as well as department chairs and other administrators.

BUILDING RELATIONSHIPS: KEEPING THE DOOR OPEN

In institutions with established information literacy programs, librarians may already enjoy a culture of collegiality and respect. Lauren Marcus, MLS, and Valerie Mittenberg, MLS, reflected about this aspect of their interaction with faculty colleagues in a recent interview: "Librarians are in demand here. We establish relationships from our participation on campus-wide committees and working groups, and never feel diminished in any way by other faculty. We participate fully in many initiatives, as well as offering professional development workshops for faculty and their own research needs. Instruction often leads to individual research consultations, which also contribute to student learning."

Librarians address time limitations in a variety of ways. When asked, Anne Deutsch, MLS, reference and instruction librarian at New Paltz, spoke of seizing an opportunity to build upon a single course-related session: "I am very conscious of the fact that time is precious, and that we must establish the value of using our services. The collaborative process is key. I will try to have a conversation with the instructor following a single session, re: how to make things better. Often the faculty member will be the one to suggest a follow-up class." Lauren Marcus told me that she uses short bursts of instruction to focus on special needs:

I sometimes conduct multiple sessions throughout the semester for some Art Studio graduate students, where I will come to them for just 15 minutes to teach something very specific, such as how to locate and find full text of journals related to their research needs. This way of working is often better than a single session devoted to a review of art resources. Instructors welcome it as well, and view it in a positive light. Where I taught in Florida, we had many online modules and instructors might select from a menu, one from column A and three from column B.

Embedding librarians within online course management systems is an increasingly popular and effective way to integrate information-seeking instruction into both in-person and distance courses.[7] Since this level of collaboration can sometimes be viewed as "invasive," participants need to have a high level of mutual trust, as well as a commitment to the time required to create assignments and respond to student queries. Later on, you will receive additional information about the embedded librarian's responsibilities in the "Online Instruction" chapter.

Service on campus committees and working groups provides excellent opportunities to work side by side with faculty outside of academic assignments. Getting to know one another in different settings can strengthen relationships. Participate in professional development opportunities at your local teaching and learning center, workshops, conferences, and symposia. These are perfect forums to not only listen to your colleagues discuss their scholarship and areas of interest, but also perhaps share some of your own.

Courses with a designated evidence-based practice or information literacy competency requirement probably schedule at least one library instruction session during the course of a semester. Volunteer for these assignments, consult with the instructor, and make yourself available for further consultations. Such relationships can lead to opportunities for more collaborative ventures.

COMMUNICATING PROFESSIONALLY: GETTING (AND KEEPING) THEIR ATTENTION

Identifying and understanding faculty needs is vital. Frequent contact has the potential of better meeting these needs and to forging a real relationship between teaching librarians and teaching faculty. "Communication plays a key role in personalized contact and in establishing channels to facilitate interaction."[8]

Conduct a survey and incorporate suggestions into your curriculum. An example of one such survey is included in figure 2.1, in which faculty were asked about preferences for incorporating library instruction into their courses. One result of this survey was discovering a number of responders who had never used the service. (Faculty were not asked to identify themselves.) A meaningful number of responders were interested in some form of "embedded" library presence, which librarians will be able to pursue as a result of the survey.

Methods of initiating contact are limited only by your imagination, your particular skills, and your talents. Librarians are smart. When asked, art liaison Lauren Marcus and a number of her colleagues contacted liaison areas using an "art card," a simple, low-tech approach, sending an oversized postcard with a catchy image appropriate to a particular area of study, with the librarian's name and personal information, along with a news update from the library on the reverse. Responses elicited the first ever instruction request from the Mathematics Department. Another request came from a member of the political science faculty who was moved to contact the librarian after seeing an art card with a 1936 New York City automat photo, which had evoked great childhood memories for him.

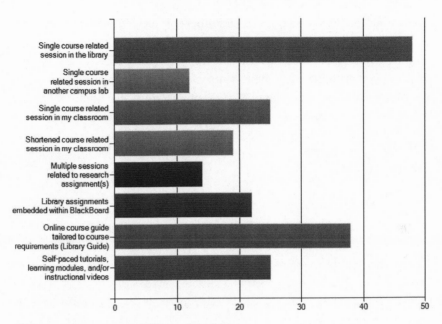

Figure 2.1. Librarian Specialties and Activities

An annual open house for new faculty (or for all faculty) or a series of informal workshops held at the beginning of each year or semester can be an excellent way to assess faculty needs and to promote library services and resources. Timing is critical, in order to reach the maximum number of participants. Such connections can lead to meaningful partnerships, but only if there is a library mind-set to "compete" with other campus events. Keeping the library and its services at the forefront is a continuing challenge. Stephan Macaluso, librarian for distance services at SUNY New Paltz, reflected upon assessing the role of the open house and similar events with the following question: "What is the value of this event and how do we sell it?" One library hosted a cocktail party for new faculty, to "connect with them [faculty] on a social level while still conveying information about library resources and services." This was so successful that it became an annual event.[9] The important thing to remember is not to be afraid to try something new.

Celebrating faculty and librarian publications or other awards also provides social reasons to get together, network, and take advantage of advocating for library instruction and other services. During an interview, outreach librarian Morgan Gwenwald pointed out the benefit of helping with library services for class use as well: "Assisting faculty with unique research opportunities for their courses has been effective. Last year, Cy Mulready (English), wanted to use items from the library's special collections for a research project, and [Morgan Gwenwald] helped with retrieving those items. Having a space in the library for students to spend multiple sessions with both the object and the professor lead to a group of outstanding online presentations."

POSITIONING THE LIBRARY: SYMBIOSIS

Library instruction is a natural platform for promoting library resources and services to everyone. Faculty members invariably learn something new each time they attend sessions with their classes. Promote services that may be of personal interest to faculty. Present professional development workshops on "Getting Your Work Published" or "Where Is My Work Cited?"

Get out of the library. Hold regularly scheduled office hours outside of the library, in areas where students are likely to be.[10] Faculty may stop to chat with you as well as students. Morgan Gwenwald suggests asking them to join you for a cup of coffee: "Meeting faculty socially and interacting outside of campus committees is a positive as well. I will invite someone out for a drink, following publication of an article or when they receive a special promotion or award." A bonus of such gestures is that they encourage faculty to advocate for the library.[11]

KNOW YOUR STUFF

In academia, this is sometimes referred to as mastery of subject matter. Knowing what you need to know in order to teach others is the teaching librarian's most powerful weapon. Keeping up with information sources, technologies, and tools gives you confidence in what you can deliver. The better you know these, the more effectively you can use them. Be sure to agree on your shared goals, by obtaining a copy of the course syllabus and understanding the assignment(s), as well as the type and amount of research required by the instructor. Nearly all classes have an online component, even if they meet face-to-face, and technological expertise adds flexibility to your delivery methods. Joe Janes, chair of the Information School at the University of Washington, emphasizes the added necessity of being "even better online than you are in person."[12]

Sit in on a class or take a course. Learn as much as you can about your liaison area, especially if this is a new or unfamiliar assignment for you. One of my colleagues spoke of sitting in on a few classes during the semester. Megan Coder, MLS, signed up for a course in basic Chinese when she took over as the library liaison to Asian Studies. Years afterward, although not fluent in Chinese, she has increased confidence pronouncing names and realizes how much her extra effort was appreciated by colleagues in the Asian Studies program. Special events, trips, or lectures are other ways to increase your knowledge or just to express interest. A liaison to geology, Morgan Gwenwald went "caving" with an instructor and his students, as part of her familiarization process with that discipline, and she loved it. As a result, she also was able to photograph the professor and a student during their field trip for a READ poster National Library Week exhibit. Stepping outside of her basic role enhanced her standing within the Geology Department and created an extremely effective visual for marketing library services.

FINAL THOUGHTS

Cooperation is a means to an end. In academia, marketing to faculty and understanding their needs is essential to the success of any instructional program. "Though librarians write about the importance of their relationship with teaching faculty, their publications more accurately demonstrate that the interest librarians have is in promoting the library, library services and information literacy."[13] Not every relationship leads to a lasting friendship, but some do, and others at least lead to collegial collaboration. With those thoughts in mind, here is a short list of 10 foot-in-the-door suggestions:

1. Have a plan. What are your goals? Discuss methods of contacting faculty that work for other teaching librarians.

2. Participate in a liaison program. Such programs enhance your status. Attend at least one departmental meeting annually and keep an eye out for other department events, participate in assessment efforts, serve on search committees, take advantage of social media.
3. Serve on committees and working groups. Consider attending faculty meetings.
4. Host library events. Examples include an open house, exhibits, National Library Week.
5. Take advantage of professional development. Participate in workshops, conferences, symposia.
6. Communicate. Send a note. Personal contact makes a difference! Examples include thank-you, congratulations, did you know . . . (Be sure to copy relevant administrators.)
7. Promote library services.
8. Assist faculty with personal research. Specifically mention services for promotion, tenure, publication, works cited, and so on.
9. Know your stuff. The more you know about a subject area, the sharper your skills operating in an online environment, the better prepared you are to meet faculty needs.
10. Become an embedded librarian. Partner within course management systems, create content, provide a library course shell for library resources, master new technologies as appropriate, answer questions.

NOTES

1. Oakleaf M. *Evidence-Based Practice for Library Instruction*. 2013. http://meganoakleaf.info/tla2011.pdf. Accessed February 13, 2014.

2. Phelps SF, Campbell N. Commitment and trust in librarian-faculty relationships: A systematic review of the literature. *J Acad Libr.* 2012;38(1):13–19.

3. Holtze T. 100 ways to reach your faculty. Presented at: Different Voices, Common Quest: Adult Literacy and Outreach in Libraries. An OLOS Preconference at the American Library Association Annual Meeting; June 13–14, 2002; Atlanta, GA. http://www.ala.org.lscsproxy.lonestar.edu/advocacy/sites/ala.org.advocacy/files/content/advleg/publicawareness/campaign@yourlibrary/prtools/academicresearch/reach_faculty.pdf. Accessed March 25, 2014.

4. Julien H, Pecoskie J. Librarians' experiences of the teaching role: Grounded in campus relationships. *LISR* 2009;31(3):149–154.

5. Badke W. Can't get no respect: Helping faculty to understand the power of information literacy. In: Kraat S, ed. *Relationships between Teaching Faculty and Teaching Librarians*. New York, NY: Haworth Press; 2005:163–177.

6. Macaluso S, Petruzzelli B. The library liaison toolkit: Learning to bridge the communication gap. In: Kraat S, ed. *Relationships between Teaching Faculty and Teaching Librarians*. New York, NY: Haworth Press; 2005: 163–177.

7. Drumm M, Havens BC. A foot in the door: Experiments with integrating library services into the online classroom. *J of Libr & Inform Serv Distance Learn.* 2005;(2)3:25–32.

8. Amante JA, Extremeno AI, Firmino da Costa A. Modelling variables that contribute to faculty willingness to collaborate with librarians: The case of the university institute of Lisbon (ISCTE-IUL), Portugal. *J Libr & Inform Sci.* 2012;(45)2:91–102.

9. Strittmatter C. If you pour it, they will come: Hosting a cocktail reception to promote services to faculty. *Public Services Quarterly.* 2008;4(3):269–276.

10. Holtze T. 3.

11. Strittmatter C. 9.

12. Janes J. What to do now and why. Slideshare website. http://www.slideshare.net/dbaaske/joe-janes. 2007. Accessed December 10, 2012.

13. Phelps SF. 2.

II

LEARNING THEORIES

3

Introduction to Learning Theories

Rebecca S. Graves and Shelly R. McDavid

It is not required to know educational theory or theorists to be an adequate instructor. However, knowing the major ones will give you a deeper understanding of the patterns and trends in education. It will deepen your knowledge of how people learn and how vexing it can be to pin down the best way to encourage or foster that learning. You can also use theories to evaluate your current teaching, thereby confirming your methods or leading you to experiment with other instructional approaches.

Knowledge of theories will enable you to build credibility as a subject expert and help to foster relationships as mentioned in earlier chapters. You will know what they are speaking of and be able to more quickly fill in gaps in your own understanding. It also helps to see the crosscurrents and contradictions that exist in higher education. This said, covering all of the major theories and theorists is beyond the scope of this chapter. For a broader overview, check out the book *Learning in Adulthood: A Comprehensive Guide* by Merriam and Caffarella.

EDUCATIONAL THEORIES/THEORISTS

John Dewey (1859–1952) is considered one of the major American educational philosophers, and his influence echoes through many threads of current society. His experience in education ranged from teaching in high schools and universities to starting his own experimental school. He was a prolific writer on a wide range of educational and philosophical topics.

Dewey held that the goal of education was to produce independent thinkers who embraced learning. He argued that schools should produce students who are reflective and moral thinkers who act on their ideas. To achieve these aims, schools should be learner focused and build on the students' real-life situations while not losing sight of the importance of the curriculum.[1] (For Dewey's educational creed, see http://en.wikisource. org/wiki/My_Pedagogic_Creed.)

Jean Piaget (1896–1980) focused primarily on development and learning in early childhood; yet, his name is so prevalent and his influence so widespread that he must be mentioned. Piaget started his studies in the natural sciences, then shifted to psychology. From his observational studies, his teaching, as well as from the study of his own children, Piaget formed his model of development. He posited that children think differently from adults, having not yet assimilated and accommodated to their world. Piaget, in his theory, proposed four stages of development: Sensorimotor (birth–2 years of age), Preoperational (2–7), Concrete Operational (7–11), Formal Operational (11–16 and onward). It is in the fourth stage that children master abstract reasoning. Piaget held that subject content should be taught to children when they are at an appropriate developmental stage. Along with Dewey, Piaget was part of the movement that placed the child, if not at the center, as an active participant in her own education. Piaget is quoted as saying "Education, for most people, means trying to lead the child to resemble the typical adult of his society . . . but for me and no one else, education means making creators. . . .You have to make inventors, innovators—not conformists."[2]

Intelligence has often been looked upon as a single ability. Howard Gardner (1943–) challenged this by identifying multiple types of intelligences.[3] Gardner identified seven types:

1. Musical
2. Bodily-kinesthetic
3. Logical-mathematical
4. Linguistic
5. Spatial

6. Interpersonal
7. Intrapersonal

Later, he added an eighth, naturalistic intelligence. The idea of multiple intelligences challenges the narrow focus on linguistics and math often found in schools. People aren't to be measured by what they know in a narrow sense—that is, what they know on a typical school test. People can be brilliant in one area and average in another.

B. F. Skinner (1904–1990) studied behaviorism or as he referred to it, radical behaviorism.[4,5] He is most widely known for his theory of operant conditioning, basically the idea that our behaviors are reactions to our environment, and those reactions are reinforced by the outcomes of the interaction. Skinner spent many years studying conditioning and reinforcement of behavior working with rats and pigeons using an instrument he designed referred to as the Skinner box. This was a machine that recorded schedules of reinforcements by recording the reactions of the animals placed inside the box. When they pressed a button in the box, they randomly received a reward. The positive reinforcement ensured that they would repeat the behavior in the future.

Skinner did not believe punishment to be an effective negative reinforcement for behavior. He held that a classroom would run smoothest with the teacher positively reinforcing the behaviors she desired—that is, not talking when the teacher is talking, paying attention, and being an active participant in one's own learning. Skinner's philosophy of operant conditioning is widely applied in classrooms today.

Malcom Knowles (1913–1997) popularized the term *andragogy*,[6] meaning adult learning, in 1970, though the term itself had been around since the 1800s. Knowles set out six principles regarding adult learning:[7]

1. Adults need to know why they are learning. (Need to know)
2. Adults prefer to be involved in managing or even designing their learning. (Self-concept)
3. The adult's prior experience should be taken into account and used in learning. (Experience)
4. Adults learn what is relevant to them, what they need to learn. (Readiness to learn)

5. Adults learn experientially and from problem solving. (Orientation)
6. Adults are internally motivated. (Motivation)

As most college and university students are considered adult, these six principles can be useful when constructing lectures and workshops, and the next chapter will cover this topic in fuller detail. Turning the six principles into questions and asking how your lesson fits with them can be an effective way to make your teaching more learner centered.

LEARNING STYLES

The idea that students have different preferences for learning and different ways in which they take in or relate to new information is familiar to many. You may tell people that you are a visual learner, preferring to learn from reading and writing, or an auditory learner, preferring to learn from listening and discussing. What you may not be aware of is the vast array of models and theories that have been put forth around learning styles since the mid-1970s. Coffield and associates identified 71 different models,[8] though many were slight variations on others, leaving only 13 major models.

This section will sample three of the learning style models, chosen as they are among the most common and also provide instruments that can be used to measure students' learning style. Note that learning styles are defined as the student's preference for how they take in or relate to new information, not their intelligence. The three styles covered here are the Dunn and Dunn Learning Style Model,[9] the Kolb Experiential Learning Theory,[10] and the VARK model.[11]

Dunn and Dunn's Learning Style Model is the most comprehensive, covering not only preferences for cognitive input but also environmental and emotional inputs. In this model, learning style is held to be fixed or innate.[12] The Productivity Environmental Preference Survey Learning Style Inventory assesses five learning style stimuli (the questionnaire is available commercially at www.humanesources.com):

1. Immediate environment (sound, light, temperature, and room design)

2. Emotionality (motivation, persistence, structure)
3. Sociological needs (learning with or without peers, with or without a teacher)
4. Physical needs (auditory, visual, tactile, kinesthetic, time of day, and mobility)
5. Psychological processing (global or analytic, hemisphericity, and impulsive or reflective)

Examples of Dunn and Dunn put into practice are alternate class schedules to give all students a day where the class is held during their peak learning time; provide casual seating such as couches and carpeted floor along with the standard tables and chairs; provide course content in different formats such as text, charts, and recordings.

Kolb's Experiential Learning Theory is based upon four styles or modes that are flexible or can change over the learner's lifetime. Kolb posits that learners range along two continuums that intersect. The first continuum is experiencing versus thinking or Concrete Experience (CE) versus Abstract Conceptualization (AC). The second continuum is doing versus reflecting, or Active Experimentation (AE) versus Reflective Observation (RO). The quadrants between the four poles create the four possible learning styles:

1. Diverger (CE/RO)—prefers concrete experience; observation over action; feeling oriented
2. Assimilator (RO/AC)—prefers theoretical models; logic more important than practicality; concerned more with ideas than people
3. Converger (AC/AE)—prefers abstract conceptualization, active experimentation; practical; nonemotional
4. Accommodator (AE/CE)—prefers active experimentation and concrete experience; intuitive; risk taker

Kolb holds that, while learners will have a preference for one quadrant or style, the best learning occurs when the learner uses all four modes sequentially. The Kolb Learning Style Inventory questionnaire is commercially available at http://learningfromexperience.com/.

The VARK strategies, developed by Neil Fleming, are one of the more popularly known learning style models. VARK stands for visual, aural/

auditory, read/write, and kinesthetic. As with other models, people range from having one strong preference to having multiple preferences. The VARK questionnaire is available online at http://www.vark-learn.com/english/index.asp. Learners who identify on the questionnaire as visual prefer charts, graphs, and design. Aural learners have a preference for discussions, asking questions, and speaking with others. Learners who fall in the read/write category prefer reading and writing. Kinesthetic learners learn best from experience and practice and by using their multiple senses.

Superficially there is commonality among the various learning styles: the premise that people vary in how they take in new information, that the student is the center of learning, and that the teacher should when possible match her teaching style(s) to the student's learning style(s). Beyond this, the models vary as to whether one's learning style is a fixed trait or a flexible preference. Also, many learning styles focus on the mental aspect of learning with only a few, such as Dunn and Dunn, including emotional and environmental preferences. There is little if any consistency on how the types of learners are defined. Fleming overlaps with Dunn and Dunn in the use of visual, aural, read/write, and kinesthetic while Kolb uses different terminology: accommodator, coverger, diverger, and assimilator. On closer comparison of Fleming and Dunn and Dunn, we see that they have divided visual to visual word and visual picture, whereas Fleming labeled those who prefer visual word as read/write. Hawk and Shah[13] as well as Coffield[14] provide more comparison on these styles.

In spite of their prevalence, there is strong criticism of learning styles in general and the instruments in particular. Budget constraints raise the question, does changing classrooms and lesson plans to mesh with learning styles actually improve educational outcomes? Research on learning styles has come up wanting.[15] Research on the reliability and validity of the instruments measuring students' styles is either inconclusive or weak, when present at all.[16] The field of neuroscience has also called into question many of the beliefs in education, the VARK learning styles being one of them. Research in this area shows that multimodal learning (e.g., seeing and hearing at the same time) is more effective than single-mode learning.[17] Using one learning style over another may not improve outcomes; however, incorporating multiple styles into your teaching can make it more interesting. Interspersing your lectures with hands-on work and incorporating discussion when possible will typically generate more involvement from the students.

LEARNING OBJECTIVES

Whether you are a guest lecturer with only 50 or 60 minutes allotted to you or the primary instructor for a semester-long course, you will have to decide on what to cover: Boolean logic, searching tips for select databases, PICO questions, copyright and correct referencing of citations—the list is long. Without clear objectives or goals, it is hard to select what topics are covered and how they are taught, and even harder to evaluate if the students have learned them. One tool to help with this is Bloom's taxonomy. Named after Benjamin Bloom (1913–1999), it is a taxonomy of educational objectives specifically for the cognitive domain.[18] The purpose of the taxonomy was to give instructors, teachers, curriculum designers, and exam writers a common vocabulary to use. *The Taxonomy of Educational Objectives: The Classification of Educational Goals* (1956) classifies cognitive learning from simple to complex, from concrete to abstract. It provides a language that educators can use to clarify and organize their objectives in their teaching and also to collaborate with other instructors, administrators, and students.

Bloom and his colleagues delineated six classes:

1.00 Knowledge
2.00 Comprehension
3.00 Application
4.00 Analysis
5.00 Synthesis
6.00 Evaluation

Each class, and any subclass, is defined and has examples given for learning objectives and test questions. For example, the novice learner starts with Knowledge, such as learning terms, definitions, and identification. She then moves up to Comprehension where she can explain, defend, and paraphrase and so on through the remaining four classes.

Verbs associated with each of the classes can easily be used to create measurable objectives. For example, if you want students to be aware that there are three major databases in their subject discipline, this would fall under Knowledge, class 1.00. Within Knowledge, *identify* and *list* are actions that show mastery of this class. The objective then would be, "The students will be able to list the three major databases." Having this statement gives you an idea of how you could structure your teaching and how you would word questions on a test. It also gives the students a clear idea of what you expect them to learn and how deeply. There are many representations of Bloom's taxonomy online, many of which provide a quick way to grasp the categories and their application to course objectives.

In 2001, Bloom's taxonomy was revised and expanded by Anderson and Krathwohl.[19] The revision shifts the list of six classes from one to two dimensions: cognitive process and knowledge. The cognitive process dimension is an adaptation of the six classes renamed and reordered as

1. Remember (knowledge)
2. Understand (comprehension)
3. Apply (application)
4. Analyze (analysis)
5. Evaluate (synthesis)
6. Create (evaluation)

The knowledge dimension covers

A. Factual knowledge
B. Conceptual knowledge
C. Procedural knowledge
D. Metacognitive knowledge

The revised taxonomy allows for more specification on the type and degree of learning sought. Be deliberate about the level of learning you expect from the students. While students should master one class (e.g., Remember) before moving on to the next class (e.g., Understand), not all subject matter needs to be learned at a deep level or at the level of mastery. Keep in mind that to truly be a master of a subject or skill takes time, thousands of hours of dedicated practice—meaning focused learning without distractions such as videos.[20] Not all students need to be masters of all that we teach. For example, a freshman does not need to know all of the databases available for accessing journal articles.

Clear, concise learning objectives can be valuable to you when working with faculty to help define both the expectations of and the time given for library instruction in their class(es). Faculty may be unrealistic about what information skills can be taught and learned within one class period. Listing out objectives for future sessions with the faculty can demonstrate the need for longitudinal curriculum-based instruction—in other words, the need for instruction over multiple classes. Therefore having longitudinal curriculum objectives can be a tool to use for advocating being integrated into the curriculum versus being a guest lecturer.

CONCLUSION

Familiarity with educational theorists will enrich your teaching by introducing you to a broader approach. Understanding how people learn will enable you to be proactive in your teaching practice and provide you with tools to utilize in your teaching, such as learning objectives. Knowledge in this area will also allow you to collaborate on a deeper level with other educators. This chapter provided a starting point on educational theory. We recommend that you continue exploring the educational theory literature.

NOTES

1. Dewey J. *The Child and the Curriculum: The School and Society.* Chicago, IL: University of Chicago Press; 1943.

2. Bringuier JC. *Conversations with Jean Piaget.* Chicago, IL: University of Chicago Press; 1980.

3. Gardner H. *Frames of Mind: The Theory of Multiple Intelligences.* New York, NY: Basic Books; 1983.

4. Gredler ME. *Learning and Instruction: Theory into Practice.* 4th ed. Upper Saddle River, NJ: Merrill; 2001.

5. Ewen RB. *An Introduction to Theories of Personality.* New York, NY: Psychology Press; 2010.

6. Knowles MS. *The Modern Practice of Adult Education: From Pedagogy to Andragogy.* Rev. ed. Chicago, IL: Association Press, Follett Publishing Co; 1980.

7. Knowles MS, Holton EF, Swanson RA. *The Adult Learner: The Definitive Classic in Adult Education and Human Resource Development.* 7th ed. Amsterdam, Netherlands: Elsevier; 2011.

8. Coffield F, Moseley D, Hall E, Ecclestone K. *Learning Styles and Pedagogy in Post-16 Learning: A Systematic and Critical Review.* London, England: Learning & Skills Research Centre; 2004.

9. Dunn RS. *Teaching Students Through Their Individual Learning Styles: A Practical Approach.* Reston, VA: Reston Publishing Co; 1978.

10. Kolb DA. *Experiential Learning: Experience as the Source of Learning and Development.* Englewood Cliffs, NJ: Prentice-Hall; 1984.

11. Fleming ND. *Teaching and Learning Styles: VARK Strategies.* 2nd ed. Christchurch, New Zealand: Neil Fleming; 2006.

12. Dunn RS. *Learning Styles: Quiet Revolution in American Secondary Schools.* Reston, VA: National Association of Secondary School Principals; 1988.

13. Hawk TF, Shah AJ. Using learning style instruments to enhance student learning. *Decis Sci J Innov Educ.* 2007;5(1):1–19

14. Coffield F. 8.

15. Pashler H, McDaniel M, Rohrer D, Bjork R. Learning styles: Concepts and evidence. *Psychol Sci Public Interest.* 2008;9(3):105–119.

16. Hawk TF, Shah AJ. Using learning style instruments to enhance student learning. *Decis Sci J Innov Educ.* 2007;5(1):1–19.

17. Geake J. Neuromythologies in education. *Educ Res.* 2008;50(2):123–133.

18. Bloom BS, Engelhart MD, Furst EJ, Walker HH, Krathwohl DR. *Taxonomy of Educational Objectives: The Classification of Educational Goals.* Vol 1. New York, NY: D. McKay; 1956.

19. Anderson LW, Krathwohl DR. *A Taxonomy for Learning, Teaching, and Assessing: A Revision of Bloom's Taxonomy of Educational Objectives.* Complete ed. New York, NY: Longman; 2001.

20. Ericsson KA. *The Road to Excellence: The Acquisition of Expert Performance in the Arts and Sciences, Sports, and Games.* Mahwah, NJ: Lawrence Erlbaum Associates; 1996.

4

Adult Learning

Christine Andresen and Katy Kavanagh Webb

The Digest of Education Statistics, published by the National Center for Education Statistics, reported that over 21 million Americans were enrolled in a degree-granting program in 2010.[1] This number is projected to rise to 24 million by the year 2020 and as depicted in figure 4.1, there is a marked historical trend toward an increase in enrollment in degree-granting institutions. For the purposes of this chapter it is important to note the projected data showing a continued upward growth of the number of adults attending college.

Instructional librarians in academic libraries are primarily concerned with the education of information literacy skills to adult learners; thus, for the purposes of this chapter, adults will be defined as any person attending library instruction who is over the age of 16.

Librarians in an academic setting are finding themselves faced not only with those students traditionally found in college classrooms, but also with students returning to school after a long absence. With these different types of adult learners attending our academic library instruction sessions, it is imperative that librarians understand the differences between these groups and the ways adult learning differs from those of children. This chapter on adult learning offers a brief overview of learning theories for adult education, as well as special considerations for library instructors to consider when designing library instruction for adult learners.

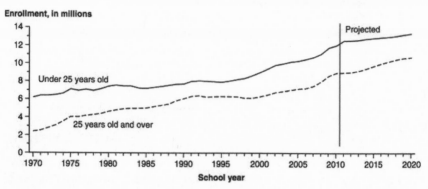

Figure 4.1.   Enrollment in Degree-Granting Institution, by Age: Fall 1970 to Fall 2020

CONSIDERATIONS OF AGE: TYPES OF ADULT LEARNERS

In most Western countries, anyone over the age of 16 is classified as an adult; however, human beings have different needs and have more life experience at various stages of their adult lives. A traditional student just entering college at 18 years of age may be away from their home and parents for the very first time, while an older adult may be juggling a job and family in addition to school responsibilities. This section of the chapter will investigate the considerations needed to educate adult learners in the vastly divergent age-related categories of traditional students, returning students, and lifelong learners.

Traditional Undergraduate Students

Traditional students are typically between the ages of 17 and 24 years old. In fact, the average age of a person in the United States seeking an undergraduate degree is 25.5 years old, showing a strong trend toward students attending college directly after high school.[2] Although no group of students is homogenous, traditional students can be categorized by having started college directly out of high school and not attending college previously. Traditional students are the youngest group of students in college and may still be maturing in body and mind. In addition to taking classes and deciding what major they would like to pursue, they are also learning valuable life lessons about living with others, navigating a new place, and pursuing interests outside of schoolwork. Thus, it may appear they are not focused on their schoolwork, but ask them and you will find that they are pledging a sorority or fraternity, enjoying making friends, or experiencing problems with a roommate. Once they have come to college, today's traditional students rely more on their parents once they have come to college than in previous generations. Keeping these traits in mind, it is important for library instructors not to rely on memories of their time as a college undergraduate. Nor is it wise to assume that students have learned academic library research in high school, even if students were in advanced placement or precollege courses.

Library instructors of traditional undergraduate students should not expect these students to be as self-sufficient as older students. When working with course instructors, it may be wise to partner with them to make sure the information you are giving them about the library is pertinent to their students' needs. Simply talking to students before the library instruction session begins will help to find out more about their specific needs and concerns. Many colleges and universities develop strong information literacy programs that are directly tied in to the university's English, writing, or communications coursework to try to reach all undergraduates. These programs work well if there are distinct learning outcomes and if those outcomes become increasingly more advanced as the students return to the library throughout the curriculum.

Returning Students

Returning students can be classified as students between the ages of 25 and retirement age. They may be enrolled as undergraduate, graduate, or professional students. Many returning students go back to school to improve their job outlook because they are unemployed, or to change their careers. It is of paramount importance that instructors recognize that returning students have varied life experiences, which may result in a more mature perspective to their studies. These students may be working in addition to attending classes, and are more likely to have children and families.[3] Certainly returning students' time is filled with different commitments than the traditional student and reflects a need for new approaches to learning.

Returning students, often referred to as nontraditional students, are usually working on their library research on nights and weekends, or when they can fit it into their busy schedules. Keep in mind that returning students may be transferring to your university, and it is likely that they may not know about library services, such as reference help and interlibrary loan. Taking part in orientations and informational fairs for distance education students, graduate students, and transfer students ensures that students will be aware of library services when needed. They may not come to the library building if they are enrolled in a distance education class, so information literacy instruction efforts need to have an online presence. In order to support these learners, it is important for instruction librarians to be flexible. If requested by instructors or students, library instructors should be willing to offer synchronous night instruction sessions using virtual classroom software. It is equally important to learn how to use screen recording and video editing software in order to offer asynchronous library courses to distance education students at the point of need. These learning objects can be embedded into the university's course management system, providing 24/7 access to information literacy tutorials.

Lifelong Learners

Lifelong learners are considered to be individuals over the age of 65. Students classified as lifelong learners are normally retired from work, but are attending school out of a strong interest in a particular subject, to learn a new skill, or due to a drive to return to school to finish a program not yet completed. In addition to these academic reasons, lifelong learners may also be participating in instruction for social interaction. Although people go back to school at every age, many colleges and universities sponsor special programs for lifelong learners, meaning that the instruction session may be a group comprised entirely of retired seniors. Many instructors find that sessions with lifelong learners are much more personal and rewarding when they foster give-and-take and thereby allow for time for students to offer their own stories. Librarians teaching lifelong learners may wish to team teach, since this group of adult learners prefers one-on-one assistance.

ADULT LEARNING THEORY:
DESIGNING INSTRUCTION FOR ADULTS OF ALL AGES

During the 20th century, the foundation of adult learning theories transformed pedagogical models of higher learning. One of the most widely known adult learning models, andragogy, will be discussed in this section. By examining the differing principles of andragogy and its humanistic roots, its potential applications in library instruction will be revealed. Applying these principles to library instruction can ultimately empower adult learners to successfully master information literacy skills.

Andragogy

Andragogy, a European concept popularized in the United States by Malcolm Knowles, is a unified concept of adult learning theory.[4] The term was originally coined to differentiate adult education from pedagogy, the art and science of helping children learn, which had become synonymous with conventional education. Several important theorists have influenced the realm of adult education and learning, including John Dewey, who believed that learning was a lifelong process based on experience.[5] Humanists Carl Rogers and Abraham Maslow were influential in defining the psychological aspects of adult learning. Rogers hypothesized that emphasizing the relevance of subject matter, providing a nonthreatening environment, and actively participating in the learning process are key components for the success of the adult learner.[6] Maslow also provided two important contributions to our understanding of adult learning. First, he emphasized the role of the adult educator in facilitating and supporting the learner and secondly, Maslow's research into human motivation included studying the motivation to learn, which has been a widely supported component of effective adult education.[7]

Principles of modern andragogy are attributed to Malcolm Knowles,[8,9] who described the learner assumptions essential to the andragogical model. These assumptions reiterate the necessity for adult educators to design instruction specifically for this unique group of learners, using a model that differs from the traditional pedagogical approach. Knowles's andragogical assumptions of adult learners are as follows:

- Adult learners need to possess a readiness to learn and understand the relevancy of knowledge being learned.
- Adult learners are self-directed; thus a lifetime of being dependent on the instructor presents a challenge, but an instructor utilizing the andragogical model can facilitate that transition.

- Adult learners are internally motivated to learn, rather than relying on external, instructor-based motivation.
- Adult learners have a wealth of personalized life experiences, which creates a need for individualized teaching methods.
- Adult learners need to actively learn using problem-based or experiential learning methodologies.[10]

In addition to describing these principles, Knowles used these assumptions to offer considerations for instructional designers to format an educational intervention for adult learners. Librarians can apply these andragogical elements to design information literacy skills training for adults.

Andragogical Implications for Library Instruction

Librarians are gradually coming to terms with the fact that traditional library instruction models are ineffective for adult learners.[11] Knowles postulates several design elements to consider in the andragogical model, all of which can be adapted to improve adult information literacy skills training. The andragogical instructor should emphasize an ideal setting that is conducive to learning, both psychologically and physically. Technology may cause anxiety for some adult learners and others may be lacking in some of the technological skills necessary to effectively master library research skills, so librarian instructors should be able to recognize signs of technostress in their adult learners. Instructors should consider speaking slowly and loudly enough to be heard or try using a microphone for students with hearing impairments. To decrease distractions, keep noise in surrounding areas to a minimum whenever possible, and use a dedicated classroom instead of having the instruction in a public area to further alleviate issues with clarity in hearing. Visual impairments can also play a factor, so make sure on-screen and printed visuals are in a font large enough to be read easily.[12] Instructors should be supportive of adult learners and encourage a climate of trust and openness, resulting in a comfortable environment of mutual respect and collaboration.

To best understand the information needs of adult learners, the library instructors should conduct a user analysis or create sample personas to become familiar with their intended audience. Personas are user profiles that can be created by conducting in-depth research on specific user types in your library, such as distance learners, undergraduate students, or lifelong learners.[13] To create a persona, the researcher collects important demographic information, which can be found in published annual institutional statistics or by questionnaires, to create generalized profiles for each learner type. Personas take the focus off of assumptions and help the instructor base decisions upon actual traits of students.

Understandably, Knowles suggests involving the learner in several phases of traditional instructional systems design models. Involving the adult learner in the needs assessment phase of the instructional design process is the best way to understand learners' information literacy performance goals. Along those same lines, Knowles[14] postulated that adult learners should work with the instructor to identify learning objectives, develop a mutually agreed upon sequence for the instruction to follow, and collaboratively devise an evaluation plan to assess the effectiveness of instruction. Library instruction can be designed with these elements in mind, collaborating with adult learners to formulate learning objectives based on their identified needs and assessing their individual outcomes as a part of the larger program evaluation. Knowles also proposes that adult learners benefit from practical, problem-based learning activities that directly address the problem the instructional intervention is intending to fix.[15] Active learning exercises have increasingly become an important part of mastering information literacy skills in higher education, so designing problem-based activities is a natural extension of current library instructional design practices.

Instruction librarians may find that professional returning students benefit from incorporating elements of evidence-based practice into their instruction. Using applicable problem-based active learning exercises will help the professional students understand the relevancy of the information, while allowing them to experience the evidence-based practice process with the librarian instructor as a facilitator. Librarian instructors can pose realistic scenarios that require professional students to develop research questions, and find appropriate evidence-based information to best answer their question. This will frame the instruction in a way that allows professional students to see the purpose of the instructional exercises and help draw connections to their real-world value.

Instructors need to be aware of different learning styles of adult learners and use each of these considerations to design information literacy instruction accordingly. Adult learners prefer to participate in instruction when it is relevant and they are not being forced into the learning environment. Instruction librarians should also consider ways to increase the adult learners' participation in training sessions and to incorporate experiential activities. During an instruction session, look for opportunities for the adult learners to practice so they can build confidence and gain self-assurance. Repetition is critical to learner understanding and should be employed to strengthen course material.[16] To firmly implant a new skill during the library instruction session, the librarian may create ways for the adult learners to teach each other. Even after utilizing these suggestions, information literacy instruction presents unique challenges to educating adult learners.

NOTES

1. Snyder TD, Dillow SA, National Center for Education Statistics. *Digest of Education Statistics 2012*. 2013;NCES 2014–015. http://nces.ed.gov/pubs2014/2014015.pdf. Accessed January 6, 2014.

2. U.S. Department of Education, National Center for Education Statistics. *The Condition of Education 2007*. 2007;NCES 2007–0064. http://nces.ed.gov/pubsearch/pubsinfo.asp?pubid=2007064. Accessed January 6, 2014.

3. Gold HE. Engaging the adult learner: Creating effective library instruction. *portal: Libr & Acad*. 2005;5(4):467-481. doi: 10.1353/pla.2005.0051.

4. Knowles MS. *The adult learner: A neglected species*. Houston: Gulf Pub. Co., Book Division; 1978.

5. Ingram DS. The andragogical librarian. *Ref Libr*. 2000;33(69/70):141-150. doi: 10.1300/J120v33n69_14.

6. Rogers CR. *Freedom to Learn: A View of What Education Might Become*. Columbus, Ohio: C. E. Merrill Pub. Co.; 1969.

7. Ingram DS. 5.

8. Knowles MS. 4.

9. Knowles MS. *Andragogy in Action*. San Francisco: Jossey-Bass; 1984.

10. Ibid.

11. Gold HE. 3.

12. Jacobson T, Williams HC. *Teaching the New Library to Today's Users: Reaching International, Minority, Senior Citizens, Gay/Lesbian, First Generation, At-risk, Graduate and Returning students, and Distance Learners*. New York: Neal-Schuman Publishers; 2000.

13. Bowles C, Box J. *Undercover user experience: Learn how to do great UX work with tiny budgets, no time, and limited support.* Berkeley, CA: New Riders; 2011.

14. Knowles MS. 9.

15. Knowles MS. 4.

16. Kenner C, Weinerman J. Adult learning theory: Applications to non-traditional college students. *J of Coll Reading & Learn.* 2011;41(2):87-96.

5

Active Learning

Barbara A. Gushrowski

WHAT IS ACTIVE LEARNING?

Active learning describes a variety of classroom instruction models that seek to engage students in their own learning. In their seminal work *Active Learning: Creating Excitement in the Classroom*, Bonwell and Eison defined active learning as "instructional activities involving students in doing things and thinking about the things they are doing."[1] Though leaders in higher education had been calling for faculty to more actively involve students in the classroom, research throughout the 1980s found that the traditional lecture method was still the predominant pedagogy across university and college campuses.[2]

Since the publication of Bonwell and Eison's report, educators have proposed a variety of active learning models developed around the common theme that learning is not a passive activity—students must be actively involved in the learning process. Thus, case-based, team-based, and problem-based learning; experiential learning; action learning; service learning; or student-centered learning models are used to engage students with the content of courses and provide opportunities for learning at a deeper level.

LEARNING THEORIES

The methods that fall under the rubric of active learning are based on long-standing learning theories, and on new findings in cognitive science about how people learn. As you recall, several learning theories were covered in the "Introduction to Learning Theories" chapter, so what follows here is a brief discussion of some theories that provide a rationale for employing active learning tools in the classroom.

Behaviorism (Doing)

Behaviorism is actually a loose collection of a number of learning theories including those of John B. Watson, B. F. Skinner (whom you read about before), and others. Three assumptions of behaviorism are that learning results in a more or less permanent change in behavior; that the environment (external stimuli), rather than the individual learner, determines what is learned; and that reinforcement of the behavior and contiguity (how close in time two events occur) are key to explaining the learning process.[3] The behaviorists emphasize observation by the instructor of the behavior of the learner and use this to measure the amount or quality of learning that has taken place. The practice of writing behavioral objectives is linked directly to this behavioral approach to measuring student learning. Behavioral objectives are developed by the instructor and specify the conditions under which the student will learn, the behavior the student will demonstrate after the learning has taken place, and the criteria by which the learning will be judged.

Active learning for the behaviorists means getting the students to do something—write, discuss, role-play, debate, and so on. Through these activities, the students demonstrate what they have learned through their reading of course materials and lectures by the instructor. Behaviorists focus much of their attention on student learning—but only learning that is observable.

Constructivism (Building)

The constructivism theory rejects the basic tenets of behaviorism that all learning is observable and that learning depends on the environment or external stimuli. Instead, constructivists propose that learners search for meaning and "create internal cognitive structures to organize their world."[4] Using this theoretical model, instructors give their students opportunities to use discussion and critical thinking activities to allow their students to add new information to existing knowledge and construct newer and deeper understanding of the content.

Cooperstein summarizes the four primary aspects of constructivism: learners *construct their own meaning*; new learning builds on *prior knowledge*; learning is enhanced by *social interaction*; and meaningful learning develops through *authentic tasks.*[5] Problem-based learning (PBL) is an example of an active learning method based on this theory of knowledge construction. The students in a PBL group (*social interaction*) are presented with a case or problem, identify what they already know (*prior knowledge*), determine what they need to know in order to understand the problem, formulate learning issues, and research the literature for answers to their questions (*construct their own meaning through an authentic task*). Thus they construct new knowledge for themselves—then return to the group to share this new information with their peers.

Cognitive Science Research

Many findings from research into how the brain works have resulted in a greater understanding of how people learn. Much of the research has been summarized and related to student learning by John Brandsford and associates in *How People Learn: Brain, Mind, Experience, and School.*[6] One concept central to the findings is an emphasis on learning with understanding. It's not enough for students to memorize a list of facts, but rather use those facts to create useable knowledge. Cognitive scientists focus on "the processes of knowing."[7] Here they agree with the constructivist view that people construct new knowledge from previous knowledge. However, an important difference is that cognitive scientists believe that teachers need to guide the students' learning and pay attention to misconceptions the students bring with them to the classroom. New knowledge can be built on faulty understandings so the teacher must play an active role in guiding the learning experience.[8]

New understanding about how people learn can lead to changes in the way we teach, what we teach, and how we assess student learning. Using active learning models in the classroom can help people take charge of their own learning, and can support learning that is transferrable to new settings and situations.

RESEARCH ON ACTIVE LEARNING

Active learning modalities enable students to engage with the content and with their learning. Students' active engagement in the teaching and learning process has been shown to be an important element in effective instruction. Dozens, if not hundreds, of studies have been conducted in the past 20 years on student learning in the context of active learning strategies employed in the classroom. Two recent reviews of the literature summarize much of this research.

Using the general definition of active learning as "any instructional method that engages students in the learning process," Prince reviewed articles on active learning, collaborative learning, cooperative learning, and PBL as the instructional methods most discussed in the literature.[9] Prince found that active learning was consistently discussed as introducing activities into a traditional lecture. Educators used a variety of methods to break up the lecture time into smaller units and allow the students opportunities to discuss, write, or think about what they'd just heard from the instructor. This method of "chunking" the content into smaller units comes from cognitive science research, which has found that student attention tends to wander after about 15 minutes of lecture. Breaking up the lecture with activities that enable students to think about, write about, and/or share their understanding of the content with the class or with a partner or small group, allows the student a rest from attending to the lecture, and following this activity, students (and the instructor) can be ready to start fresh again.[10]

Prince summarizes the findings of several studies about student engagement into three focal points: activity, collaboration, and cooperative learning. "Introducing activity into lectures can significantly improve recall of information while extensive evidence supports the benefits of student engagement."[11] Collaboration "enhances academic achievement, student attitudes, and student retention,"[12] and cooperative learning enhances "interpersonal skills . . . and . . . cooperation is more effective than competition for promoting a range of positive learning outcomes . . . including . . . enhanced academic achievement."[13]

Michael investigates the writings from the learning sciences, cognitive science, and educational psychology. He summarizes key findings from these areas of research:

- Learning involves the active construction of meaning by the learner.
- Learning facts and learning to do something are two different processes.
- Some things learned are domain specific—other things are more readily transferred to other domains.
- Individuals are likely to learn more when they learn with others than when they learn alone.
- Meaningful learning is facilitated by articulating explanations to one's self, peers, or teachers.[14]

Both authors address the impediments or road blocks to implementing active learning in the classroom. Michael warns that "active learning doesn't just happen."[15] Faculty development is key to the success of implementing any new approach to teaching. These strategies often take more prep time and can be daunting when tried the first time, and the unpredictability of the outcomes can be intimidating and frightening. The concern that less content will be delivered causes faculty to shy away from any classroom activity that does not involve delivery of content to the student through the lecture.

ACTIVE LEARNING ACTIVITIES

Much of the instruction conducted by librarians is by its very nature active. Librarians realized long ago that deeper learning takes place when the students are able to actively take part in the instruction rather than passively viewing a presentation. Instruction in the use of databases, for example, lends itself well to an active learning activity. Following is a brief introduction to active learning methods and activities that you can use to get students involved in their learning. These can be used in large or small classes and in-person or online classes. Some require an investment in technology, others do not. Several of these are discussed in greater detail in subsequent chapters in this book. Key to implementing any teaching method or strategy is to tie the activities to the learning objectives for the course. Not all of these activities are suited to all courses, so find one or two that you are comfortable implementing.

Flipped Classroom

In this model the students are assigned readings, videos, or other work to be completed outside the classroom prior to the class meeting. The in-class session is then used to discuss or review the pre-class work. This method can improve student learning and understanding of content by testing the students' knowledge and understanding and clearing up misconceptions prior to a summative exam. Specific activities might include having students prepare multiple-choice questions based on the readings and post these to you prior to the start of class. This gives you a sense of what content the students may be having problems with and you can adjust your class time to cover those concepts in more detail. You can also use these questions to give a clicker quiz or do a small-group quiz among the students.

Blended Learning

The course is delivered as a blend of online and face-to-face instruction.[16] In a blended learning environment, the students are held accountable for learning outside the classroom. This is another way to "flip" the classroom and provides some flexibility for the students to work on the material on their own time schedule. The structure of the online component can also provide opportunities for collaborations among and between the students since they are not impeded by time and space constraints. Blended learning is a concept that will be covered in more depth in a later chapter.

Problem-Based Learning

There are many ways to construct a PBL curriculum or course, but in most forms, the students are divided into small groups and are given a problem to work through. They work through this problem by creating concept maps of hypotheses about the problem; discussing and reviewing their existing knowledge related to the problem; then identifying gaps in their knowledge that will require additional research in order to gain deeper understanding of the problem. Following the research portion of the process, the students present to their group their research findings and their new understanding of the issues identified during the initial discussion. The ultimate goal of PBL is that students develop and refine critical thinking skills, learn how to identify their information needs, and learn how to learn.

The PBL model can be used with library instruction in a number of ways depending on the time allotted. For a short session or a one-shot session, the students are asked to bring a research problem or question to the class. It will be helpful to collaborate with the instructor, who can help the students develop the topics around the goals of the course. The students can be paired or grouped into small groups and brainstorm a list of things they know about the topic and a list of what they don't know and want or need to know. The librarian than can introduce the students to an article database or collection of online textbooks where the students are likely to find the answers. When the students develop the learning issues and questions, they are more engaged in learning how to use the database to find the information they are seeking. There may not be enough time in the session for the students to read about their topic and discuss the merits of the information—but at the end of the session, they can be asked to reflect on the process of using the database to find articles on their topic. If the library instruction extends over several sessions, the students will have more opportunities to discuss and reflect on the ease or difficulty of finding appropriate information, work on rephrasing their question and developing alternate search terms, discuss the pros and cons of the database they used, and learn about other databases. There can also be instruction and discussion about the reliability, relevance, and levels of confidence students have in the information resources they are using.

Clickers

These gadgets have been found to be especially effective as a way to engage large classes. The instructor prepares slides that query the students on key concepts from that day's lecture or pre-class readings. Students use the clickers to answer the questions electronically, the votes are tallied, and the instructor can quickly gauge the class's understanding of important concepts. Clickers allow students to respond without the pressure of speaking out in class when they are unsure of the answer. Some faculty set up the clickers so that individual students can be identified (by the instructor); they can be held accountable for attendance and/or participation as well as their understanding. Students have to think through their own answers before finding out how everyone else responded. Frequent and immediate feedback that the clicker can provide has been shown to be effective for student learning.[17] You'll read more about this topic in the "Audience Response Systems" chapter.

Think-Pair-Share

This method was developed by Frank Lyman at the University of Maryland in 1981. The three-step process works with any size class. The instructor poses a question or problem and then each student thinks about the problem, pairs with another student to further discuss, and then the pair share with the class their thoughts or solutions.[18]

SUMMARY

Active learning is not a new concept, nor is it a method that guarantees all students will learn more. What it does do is refocus attention from teaching (faculty) to learning (student). Any activity undertaken in the classroom should be done with the course/class objectives in mind. Don't do something just to get the students active—do something active that enables the students to learn. There is a growing body of evidence that applying some active learning methods can enhance student learning. How many of these methods you apply and how often will be guided by the course objectives, your comfort level with the activity, and the authenticity of the activity to achieve course objectives. Start with one activity—if it works, great; if it doesn't, try something else. Mix it up—do a little or do a lot. Just keep the learning objectives in mind: the activity should help the students attain the knowledge or skills desired.

NOTES

1. Bonwell CC, Eison JA. *Active Learning: Creating Excitement in the Classroom*. ASHE-ERIC higher education report. Washington DC: School of Education and Human Development, George Washington University, 1991.

2. Ibid.

3. Merriam SB, Caffarella RS, Baumgartner L. *Learning in Adulthood: A Comprehensive Guide.* 3rd ed. The Jossey-Bass Higher and Adult Education Series, San Francisco, CA: Jossey-Bass, 2007.

4. Baumgartner LM, et al. Adult Learning Theory: A Primer. Information Series, 2003.

5. Cooperstein SE, Kocevar-Weidinger E. Beyond active learning: A constructivist approach to learning. *Ref Serv Rev.* 2004;32(2):141–148.

6. Bransford J, et al. *How People Learn: Brain, Mind, Experience, and School.* National Academy Press: Washington DC, 2000.

7. Ibid.

8. Ibid.

9. Prince M. Does active learning work? A review of the research. *J Eng Educ.* 2004;93(3):223–231.

10. Ibid.

11. Ibid.

12. Ibid.

13. Ibid.

14. Michael J. Where's the evidence that active learning works? *Adv Physiol Educ.* 2006;30(4):159–67

15. Ibid.

16. Garrison DR, Kanuka H. Blended learning: Uncovering its transformative potential in higher education. *The Internet and Higher Educ.* 2004;7(2):95–105.

17. Keough SM. Clickers in the classroom: A review and a replication. *J Manag Educ.* 2012;36(6):822–847.

18. Anderson FT. *Mainstreaming Digest: A Collection of Faculty and Student Papers.* College Park: University of Maryland, 1981.

FURTHER READING

Bonwell CC, Eison JA. *Active Learning: Creating Excitement in the Classroom.* ASHE-ERIC higher education report. Washington DC: School of Education and Human Development, George Washington University, 1991.

Svinicki MD. *McKeachie's Teaching Tips: Strategies, Research, and Theory for College and University Teachers.* 13th ed. Belmont, CA: Wadsworth, Cengage Learning, 2011.

Fink LD. *Creating Significant Learning Experiences: An Integrated Approach to Designing College Courses.* Rev. ed. San Francisco, CA: Jossey-Bass, 2013.

III

INSTRUCTIONAL TECHNIQUES

6

Introduction to Instructional Techniques

Rebecca S. Graves and Shelly R. McDavid

Now that you have learned about different roles librarians take in the curriculum and how to go about building relationships, it is time to start teaching. This chapter has been written to provide a basic tool kit to allow you to be more comfortable in the classroom and to speak more knowledgably with faculty and instructional designers at your institution. Also, it is intended as a grounding upon which you can build your knowledge and skill as an instructor.

METHODS OF INSTRUCTION

For the purpose of this chapter, we segment teaching into four main methods: lecture, discussions, readings, and exercises (including experiments and projects). Each of these four can be expanded or defined more specifically; for example, we place demonstrations under lecture and writing papers under exercises. Student presentations would also fall under exercises, though the presentations might cross over into lecture.

How to use these four methods depends on the following conditions: your role in the course, the context, the content, and the classroom. If your role is the primary instructor, you have the authority to assign grades. You also have time and continuity with the students. Methods such as readings or projects work better if the teacher and students meet multiple times over a course of weeks. If you are a guest lecturer, you will most likely not be assigning grades or giving outside assignments. Therefore, the methods you choose will need to fit within the framework of that one class. One way to expand your options is to work on the relationship with the faculty member who invited you to speak to her or his class. When you have a strong collaboration and understanding with the faculty member, she or he may well be willing to assign a reading or exercise that you suggest.

Why the students need to know the information, or the context of the course, determines your objectives. Referring to Bloom's taxonomy, freshman students in an introductory course may only need to remember factual knowledge such as the website for the library and the name of one or two main databases. In this case, a brief demonstration or lecture might be the best teaching method. Another class, say sophomores who will be writing a research paper, will need to apply procedural knowledge. In their case a lecture would not be sufficient for them to learn the skills they need. Combining hands-on exercises along with demonstration will increase the impact of your teaching for these students.

Content will also play a role in which teaching method you choose. Clarify with the faculty member what her or his objectives are, then brainstorm from your expertise what the students need. Once you have worked these ideas through Bloom's taxonomy to form objectives, you will be close to having the content of what you will be sharing with the students. If the content is how to use databases to find sources for a research project, then exercises and demonstrations, as mentioned earlier, work well. If the content is how to avoid plagiarism, a discussion in the class might make a stronger impression than a straight-up lecture.

Finally, no matter how much thought you have given to the learning objectives or how much of a roll you have in the course, you will be constrained by the classroom and the equipment available. Hands-on exercises at a computer might be the best method for a particular course, but you may not be able to use this method if a computer lab is not available or the students cannot bring their own. Classrooms where the chairs are bolted to the floor in rows can make discussions difficult. This highlights the importance of knowing the room that you will be teaching in well in advance so that you can make allowance for the equipment or lack thereof.

Taking your objectives and context and setting them down in a step-by-step lesson plan allows you to focus on your students and their learning rather than on remembering what comes next. Having a written plan will help you with your pacing and tracking of time and will be especially useful on those days when technology doesn't work or other problems crowd in on your teaching. This holds true whether you are a guest lecturer or the primary instructor.

Lesson plans can follow a strict format or a simple outline. Whichever form you choose, begin with the objectives that you determined for the class and introduce them and yourself to the class. Note in your plan what activities you will have the students do along with time estimates for each section. Plan your ending. It is good to practice what you will say to indicate to the students that you are done and they are free to leave. Examples of lesson plans and outlines can be found online and by contacting colleagues.

PRESENTATION SKILLS

You can be solid in your subject knowledge, a known scholar of educational theory, and have beautiful, elegant learning objectives and the perfect methods for teaching them. Yet, if your performance in the classroom—online or face-to-face—shuts the students down, all of your work and preparation is for naught. The key here is "performance." There are many similarities between teaching and acting: the use of voice and body, props, a stage, and timing.[1] Taking tips from the world of theater can improve your teaching.

Starting with your voice, make sure to use dynamic range. Speak loudly enough for all the students to hear, yet also vary the dynamics. Lower your voice slightly in a key section to encourage the students to lean in, to listen more closely. Listen to your voice to find if you are supporting it with enough breath. When we don't breathe deeply or often enough, our voices can sound raspy or squeaky, which is unpleasant to listen to and often sends the unwanted message that we are anxious. In a private place, practice your breathing and speaking. Try warming up with tongue twisters or other vocal exercises, such as laughing at different pitches. If that is too much, simply practice delivering some of your lecture making sure to support your voice with enough breath. One benefit of this will be to slow down your speaking as we often speak too fast when teaching. A second benefit will be to give your voice more command or authority. If you are teaching online listen to your voice in the recordings or have a colleague attend your session and report back on how you used your voice.

Your body is also instrumental in your performance. Pay attention to your posture, with the goal being to stand straight and relaxed. Also check your use of gestures. Think of gestures as part of your teaching to guide the students' attention and focus.

Timing is another key element of stage performance. Like actors or comedians, instructors can also use pauses and changes in the tempo of their speech and body movement. Especially when using questions to elicit interaction and deeper learning from students, you can slow down, pause, and allow the students time to form their thoughts. You can vary the pacing not only of your speech but also of the activities that you do in class.

All of performing takes place in space. The classroom is your set, and laser pointers, notes, handouts, and markers are some of the props. Knowing your scenery, such as the projector, the whiteboard, the layout of the room, or the online courseware, will assist you in being more relaxed and better able to concentrate on teaching and communicating with the students. Being comfortable and practiced with your props, online or physical, reduces the chances of them becoming a distraction. Also, if you know the props and set you are less likely to be overwhelmed when a malfunction happens and more likely to think of a work-around.

A final connection between teaching and performing is practice. It is generally assumed that actors rehearse before their performance and specifically rehearse with the set and props that they will be using. As a teacher, you will also benefit from rehearsing and practicing even if it is for a few minutes. To get the most out of the practice, make it as close as possible to the actual instruction. If you can go to the classroom, do so and use the equipment and practice speaking out loud and using the room as you plan to during class. If you do not have access to the classroom, simply standing at your desk while you go through your class outline or script will benefit your performance.

ASSESSING YOUR TEACHING

As with any performance, feedback and coaching will make yours better. Enlist a colleague to assess the effectiveness of your teaching methods.

Such peer evaluations can be integral to the improvement of your teaching practice. There are many resources online, even free peer evaluation forms that can be helpful to this process.[2] To make the most of the evaluation, meet with your peer before the class to provide him or her with background information such as the syllabus, the pre-work done by the students to prepare for this class, what the instructor wants the students to learn, how this information fits with the overall course, as well as any other specific aspects the instructor would like feedback on. After the class, schedule a post-observation meeting where your peer provides you with specific and actionable information on your strengths and weaknesses. A benefit of peer evaluations is that you and your evaluator can decide the specific variables that will be examined.

Another option for feedback is to record your lectures/classes. Video recordings can show your posture and use of gestures as well as how you use your voice. If that is not possible, audio recordings will give you feedback on your pacing and speaking.

Finally, make use of your students. At the end of class you can ask them to write down what specifically was useful in the class and what specifically could be improved. This can be done on paper or online. Paper or 3×5 cards have the benefit of being quick and getting good participation rates, but an online form will save you from having to retype or file cards and slips of paper.

MANAGING INSTRUCTION MATERIALS

Use consistent file paths and include them in the footer of your document. Instruction generates documents. Whether you are the sole instructor or you work with a team, taking time to set up a filing system will avoid a crisis down the road. For example, if an instructor asks you to teach on short notice, being able to quickly retrieve previous notes and outlines can mean the difference between having to cancel or being able to fit the class in. The filing system doesn't have to be complex; in fact, a simple system means you'll be more likely to use it. Create a dedicated folder for your materials and then choose headings for each type of document, such as "outline" or "lecture notes." What the headings are matters less than that they make sense to you or your team and that you consistently apply them.

If you have paper copies, it is helpful to place the file path in the footer field to make it easy to find the master digital file. If you share teaching duties consider having a standard template for your handouts protocols for including the creator's initials and date created or revised. Should you have need of a physical filing system, Sue Stigleman provides a workable, simple model.[3] Once you have your system in place, make sure that the files are backed up on a periodic basis. If you work at a large institution, this may be done for you. If not, set a calendar to back up on a quarterly basis. Paper files can be weeded on a yearly basis.

CONCLUSION

Planning and practice are essential if you seek to become an excellent instructor. What you will teach your students and why it is important. The methods you choose to present the information should be based on their needs. We have outlined the basics of instruction techniques with the intention that it is a starting point for exploring and learning about this subject.

NOTES

1. Timpson WM, Burgoyne S. *Teaching and Performing: Ideas for Energizing Your Classes.* 2nd ed. Madison, WI: Atwood Publishers; 2002.

2. Cornell University Center for Teaching Excellence. Peer review of teaching. 2012. http://www.cte.cornell.edu/resources/documenting-teaching/peer-review-of-teaching/index.html. Updated April 11, 2014. Accessed July 2, 2014.

3. Stigleman S. Organizing information management education materials. *Med Ref Serv Q.* 1991;10(3):61–66.

7

Audience Response Systems

Emily M. Johnson

Librarians providing instruction know the challenge of gauging prior knowledge or understanding of key concepts, and engaging and encouraging students' participation during an instruction session. Throughout this chapter, you will be introduced to audience response systems (ARS) as a way to address some of these challenges as well as learn about some of the different technology available, strategies for implementation, and best practices.

INTRODUCTION TO AUDIENCE RESPONSE SYSTEMS

Libraries and higher education have seen a great increase in ARS use to assist in instruction during the past decade. ARS is an electronic service or application that allows participants to enter multiple-choice, true/false, or free-form questions posed in real-time during a class.[1] Other commonly used names in the literature include classroom response system, classroom performance system, open-ended response system, personal response system, student response system, and the colloquial term *clicker*. With the use of this educational technology, instructors have the opportunity to engage and assess, both formatively and summatively, student involvement in learning objectives for an instructional session. With target questioning, ARS can impact specific learning domains, making a traditionally passive, one-way communication lecture or instruction session a

more engaging and fun experience.[2] ARS offers potential solutions to issues posed in librarian-lead instruction, including assessment of learning,
student engagement, instructor/student barriers, student fear, and so on.

ARS developed out of a need for the military to gain feedback from
their students during review of filmed instructional materials back in the
1960s.[3] These systems grew in popularity, expanding beyond education
to businesses using them for focus groups, employee training, and meetings.[4] In the 1990s, the wired systems were replaced with clickers, a
"pared-down TV remote control unit."[5] This transformation into a more
accessible technology leads to widespread adoption in higher education,
including libraries. In the past few years, ARS applications are now being built for use on mobile devices. While the technology systems might
have changed, most of the available research can be applied to any ARS
technology.

Extensive bibliographies on ARS use are available from the Center for
Teaching at Vanderbilt University,[6] the UW-System Clicker project,[7] and
the UBClicks project from the University of Buffalo,[8] to allow instructors
to learn more about this technology.

INCLUDING ARS IN LIBRARY INSTRUCTION

Integrating ARS into the classroom provides instructors the opportunity
to promote active learning and assessment. Gaining students' opinions,
attention, and immediate feedback allows instructors to adjust instruction sessions to the needs of the students, no matter what the size of the
class. This can be accomplished with ARS activities like pre-/posttest-
ing, comprehension checks, and questions prompting student discussion
in instruction sessions. With these activities, even shyer students are
more apt to participate, lowering the inherent barrier between student
and instructor.

Collecting responses to verbal assessment questions is challenging,
as they are almost never graded and are often anonymous[9] in the library
instruction setting. But with the ability of ARS, instructors are able to use
captured response data to show the resulting impact on student learning.
Through targeted questioning, librarians are able to capture existing information literacy knowledge of students, which can then demonstrate the

need for information literacy instruction sessions and programs.[10] While it has been argued in the literature how impactful pre-/posttesting and immediate feedback with ARS are to student learning outcomes or the long-term information-seeking behavior,[11,12] many studies in library settings have suggested ARS is more effective than lecture alone.[13,14,15]

While it can be difficult to engage students in library instruction sessions, ARS has the potential for allowing students to be responsible for their own learning by prompting with questions. Instructors using ARS strongly advocate that students who commit to an answer, even if they guess, are invested in the questions and will pay better attention to the discussion that follows.[16] Whether integrating this technology into an evidence-based mini-curriculum,[17] an invited lecture series,[18] or a one-shot instruction session,[19,20] ARS offers the chance of for a more fun and interactive, student-centered instruction session.

Large lectures are often intimidating and make it difficult for student/teacher connections. ARS lowers the inherent barriers between students and instructors by allowing direct response to instructor inquiry. Speaking in front of peers is often intimidating for students and ARS offers the solution of anonymity when responding, allowing for students to feel comfortable volunteering answers to even controversial topics.[21,22] According to Graham and associates, self-identified reluctant students "perceived [ARS instruction strategies] that provided formative feedback and empowered them to evaluate their own performance."[23]

ARS TECHNOLOGY

With many available ARS instruction opportunities, it is important to know what systems are available to instructors. ARS technology continues to evolve with many different services and technological capabilities. Based on two interfaces, the instructor and student, ARS requires two devices to function—the input devices for students and the device running the program collecting responses for the instructor. When the polling activity is complete, the responses can be displayed on a projection screen, either in a graphical or listed format. Currently, there are two main ARS options—the hardware-required system or the web-based system. Both have similar functionality but differ in device and response collection.

The device used for response submission is dependent on the system being used. The program used to coordinate ARS serves the function of designing and administering questions. To select the most appropriate system, it is important to review the features and apply them to the needs in the instruction classroom. Important factors to consider include type of instruction, choice of device, customizable features, the cost of the system, and technical support for the product.

Hardware-based systems are based on use of the clicker, a handheld input device about the size of a television remote, usually with a 10-digit numeric or 5-point alphabetic keypad. The student can submit answers by clicking on the button, transmitting a unique infrared or radiofrequency signal. Instructors using hardware-based ARS must be cognizant of the extra expense of $25–$60USD students might incur if requiring a clicker purchase. The proprietary hardware-based ARS software often allows for multiple features and customization, including identifying student responses, assigning point values to answers, and "add-in" or exporting ability, integrating with programs like slide presentation software or a response grade spreadsheet to follow learning management systems. The software program is often offered for little to no cost for an institution implementing hardware-based ARS across a campus. Table 7.1 (adapted and updated from Connor[24]) contains several hardware-based ARS options available.

Table 7.1.   Hardware-Based ARS Vendors

Vendor	Software Product(s)	Website
eInstruction Corporation	Insight360 & CPS (classroom performance software)	http://www.einstruction.com
TurningTechnologies	TurningPoint and ResponseWare	http://www.turningtechnologies.com
H-ITT	MultiPoint software	http://www.h-itt.com
iClicker	iClicker software	http://www.iclicker.com
iRespond	iRespond Teacher's Dashboard	http://www.irespond.com
Promethean	ActivEngage	http://www.prometheanworld.com
Qwizdom	Connect and Actionpoint softwares	http://www.qwizdom.com
Smart Technology, Inc.	SMART Response	http://www.smarttech.com

The web-based ARS is dependent on the BYOD, or "bring your own device," model. Students' access to the technology has previously been a concern with this model; however, with smartphone ownership up to 55% and laptop computer ownership up to 61% of American adults,[25] this concern continues to shrink. Web-based ARS programs are based in the cloud, not requiring downloaded software, only an Internet connection. While many are not as robust in the customizations or features as the hardware-based counterparts, the majority are free to use, at their base-level of service. Often with limited capability to record students' individual answers or to integrate into other programs, the web-based system might not fulfill the needs of a semester-long course using ARS to calculate student participation or quizzes. A few of the more robust options offer fee-based levels of service to accommodate larger classes, more responses, student registration, and point values. Another concern includes accessibility to Wi-Fi and mobile networks; not all instruction locations will have the networking capabilities needed for a web-based system. Table 7.2 contains several web-based ARS options available.

INTEGRATING ARS INTO INSTRUCTION

As instructors, designing effective questions is more difficult than the use of ARS technology. It is essential to remember ARS is the technological

Table 7.2. Web-Based ARS Vendors

Vendor	Website
ClassPager	http://www.classpager.com
Flisti	http://www.flisti.com
Geddit	http://www.letsgeddit.com
GoSoapBox	http://www.gosoapbox.com
InfuseLearning	http://www.infuselearning.com
Kahoot!	https://getkahoot.com
Mentimeter	http://www.mentimeter.com
PoLLCODE	http://www.pollcode.com
PollEverywhere	http://www.polleverywhere.com
QuestBase	http://www.questbase.com
QuizBean	http://www.quizbean.com
Quizdini	http://teach.quizdini.com
Socrative	http://www.socrative.com

vehicle for questioning during an instruction session and should be used with solid pedagogical foundations. Questioning during instruction can deliberately aid and increase learning, if the questions are well designed and target a higher order of thinking, not just promoting memorization or demonstrating rote learning. It involves a great amount of effort and practice to master designing effective questions.

When using ARS, the questions are typically written prior to the instruction session during lesson planning. This does not mean questions cannot be added during the session, especially "when hit by sudden inspiration, concern about student understanding, or a question from a student that could be addressed by the class as a whole."[26] With practice and experience, instructors can even start to anticipate questions students will ask during a session.

Instructors can build questions to

- Increase or manage interaction
- Assess student preparation and ensure accountability
- Find out more about students
- Guide formative assessment
- Guide thinking, review, or teach
- Make lectures fun[27]

By thinking of these common purposes for ARS use, integrating into instruction is only limited to the imagination. To design effective questions, instructors need to start with accomplishable learning outcomes, utilizing appropriate question formats and types to target relevant learning domains.

QUESTION TAXONOMY

Question development starts with the preparation of sound learning outcomes. A learning outcome is a statement of what students will learn in the instruction session, focusing on student learning rather than instructor teaching. They include a stem (who is attending the class), a verb phrase reflecting a learning domain from an educational taxonomy (i.e., Bloom's), and a product that is the students' response to the question.

Bloom's taxonomy is the most widely adopted model of cognitive levels.[28] You may remember reading about this in chapter 3. Writing questions for the lower levels of knowledge or comprehension is relatively easy as they focus on facts and explaining material meaning. Moving up the learning levels to either synthesis or evaluation is much more difficult; it involves creating something new or the critique of something established. Learning outcomes can be developed from discipline-based objectives such as the ACRL (Association for College and Research Libraries) Information Literacy Standards, AAMC (Association of American Medical Colleges) Medical School Objectives Project, or instructor-set objectives from course work. After defining the learning outcomes, questions can be formulated to aid in student engagement and assessment.

CONTENT QUESTIONS

Content questions are used to directly assess student learning by focusing on the content of an instruction session and having right or wrong responses.[29] Through the question results, the instructor can change the session's dynamics and content by reviewing responses from all the students. Content questions have three categories: recall, conceptual understanding, and application questions.

Recall questions are used in a class session to ask students to remember facts, concepts, or procedures relevant to the session's objectives. They do not assess student understanding, only their memory of the facts, concepts, or procedures. Since they do not generate discussion, they are not typically used as student engagement. If you are teaching multiple library instruction sessions, you can use recall questions at the beginning of an instruction session to test students' recall of basic facts prior to moving to activities with a need of deep understanding and comprehension. Connor, in the article "Using Cases and Clickers in Library Instruction: Designed for Sciences Undergraduate," uses a multiple-choice recall question by having students define "empirical evidence"; she later builds onto student understanding of empirical evidence by asking questions using concept and application questions.[30]

The conceptual understanding questioning type involves not only recalling information but also understanding the concept presented.[31] By listing common misunderstandings with the correct answer, the instructor addresses misunderstandings within important concepts and even engages students in discussion. One example of a question framework in the literature of conceptual understanding questions is the Concept Test by Eric Mazur of Harvard University. In Mazur's physics courses, he uses this "effective method which teaches the conceptual underpinning and leads to better student performance on conventional problems."[32] The following framework is timed to allow for students think about the concept or process to justify their answer:[33]

1. Question posed (one minute)
2. Students given time to think (one minute)
3. Students record individual answers (optional)
4. Students convince their neighbors/peer instruction (one to two minutes)
5. Students record revised answers (one minute)
6. Feedback to teacher: tally of answers (one minute)
7. Explanation of correct answer (two-plus minutes)

Based on this formula, each question asked can take around five minutes of lecture time; however, the format is adaptable time-wise to proceed quickly through a concept if students understand or to supplement with more lecture if a student percentage needs more concept coverage.

Application questioning strives to achieve higher levels of cognition. The students have to apply their knowledge and understanding to concrete scenarios, which are used from real life, textbook examples, or national board exams. Bruff explains, "Application questions are useful for encouraging integrative learning: learning in which students make connections among ideas . . . across the boundary between academic setting and the real world."[34] Bombaro provides an example of asking true/false application questions in a library instruction scenario in the article "Using Audience Response Technology to Teach Academic Integrity: 'The Seven Deadly Sins of Plagiarism' at Dickinson College." She asks students to identify plagiarism from samples of plagiaristic writing after finding some students who correctly answered earlier true/false recall questions about plagiarism were not able to address the application-orientated questions correctly.[35] By designing effective questioning, she was able to address the issue and help the students work through a more "real-world" scenario.

PROCESS QUESTIONS

While instructors want to know if students comprehend presented content, they should also be concerned if they are engaging with the content. Process questions are used to gather information from students to help shape students' interactions with each other and class content, providing their opinion, experiences, and confidence in their knowledge.[36] These questions allow for exploration of the affective domain that is as important as the cognitive domain. This can help instructors intervene when a student may have given up or may be facing library-related anxiety.[37] Two main types of process questions are student perspective and monitoring questions.

Student perspective questions allow for students to share their opinions and personal experiences, allowing for instructors to learn more about their students and tailor learning experience for the unique makeup of students. This also prevents instructors from making unfounded assumptions about student knowledge. An example of this type of questioning would be to start out a class session asking the students about their experiences with searching scholarly literature. Through their responses, the instructor can help students see the relevance of a session's objectives to their needs.

Monitoring questions can be integrated into an instruction session when an instructor wants to know the students' confidence levels of their understanding of the content. This type of process questioning can be helpful when reviewing content to monitor the student's learning experience. This model has frequently been utilized with Twitter to provide a back channel of feedback[38] or as a Muddiest Point activity to help assess students' difficulty with an unclear or confusing component in a presentation.[39] This could easily be done with ARS using either a multiple-choice Likert scale question or a short-answer response.

QUESTION FORMATS

After thinking about the learning objectives and question types, question design is also dependent on the structure of the question. By choosing an appropriate question format, it will help in designing and interpreting question responses. When using ARS, the instructor must be aware of

Table 7.3.   ARS Questions Formats Advantages and Disadvantages

Question Format	Advantages	Disadvantages
Multiple Choice	• Use for many kinds of subject matter and learning outcomes • Easy to score	• Hard to write for higher levels in the cognitive domain
True/False	• Easy to write/score • Scoring is objective	• Measures only low levels of cognitive learning • Encourages guess because of only two alternatives
Matching	• Easy to write/score	• Does not measure any interpretation, judgment, or application • Students can use rote memorization to answer
Short Answer	• Easy to write • Reduces possibility of guessing • Can discriminate achievement effectively	• Can be a measure of memorization ability • Interpretation is subjective

question formats available for that specific system. Common formats that can be accommodated by ARS are multiple-choice, true/false, matching, or short-answer questions. When designing questions, there are several advantages or disadvantages of the individual question formats, shown in table 7.3 (adapted from Penn State University Intro to Writing Questions Learning Object).[40]

BEST PRACTICES AND SOLUTIONS TO BARRIERS ENCOUNTERED WITH ARS

It is important to weigh the potential benefits and barriers of integrating ARS into instruction. In a study done by Nielsen and associates looking at teacher-centric aspects of ARS use, students gave feedback on how the technology was integrated into their instruction session. They expressed concerns with technology failure, instructor experience with the technology, and how instructors practice and prepare for the use of ARS.[41] ARS can also be a financial investment for instructors and students, depending on the system.[42] To help in offsetting the costs, there are many education technology grants available in higher education for librarians to apply for funding to purchase both licenses and equipment for ARS use.

Many papers have been produced in the literature consisting of best practices and tips when using ARS in instruction.[43,44] Some of those tips include the following:

- Keep the focus on pedagogy—not the technology.
- Design questions with a specific learning goal.
- Keep questions and instruction clear, short, and focused.
- Build in at least five minutes per question activity to allow for peer discussion.
- Plan for contingency teaching in case of technological failure.
- For invited instruction sessions, ask instructor if he or she has implemented an ARS already; don't make students learn a new ARS if they are not already familiar with one.

The use of ARS to improve teaching and learning is dependent on the instructor using sound pedagogical principles. ARS technology can enliven teaching practice and allow students to become invested in the learning process. By addressing major deficits of engagement and assessment in instruction sessions, ARS is "a powerful and flexible tool for teaching."[45]

NOTES

1. EDUCAUSE Learning Initiatives. 7 things you should know about open-ended response systems. http://www.educause.edu/library/resources/7-things-you-should-know-about-open-ended-response-systems. Created February 12, 2011. Accessed April 11, 2014.

2. Caldwell JE. Clickers in the large classroom: Current research and best-practice tips. *CBE-Life Sci Educ*. 2007;6(1):9–20. doi: 10.1187/cbe.06-12-0205.

3. Sawada D. Learning from past and present: Electronic response systems in college lecture halls. *J of Comput Math & Sci Teach*. 2002:167–181.

4. Collins LJ. Livening up the classroom: Using audience response systems to promote active learning. *Med Ref Serv Q*. 2007;26(1):81–88.

5. EDUCAUSE Learning Initiatives. 1.

6. Bruff D. Classroom response system ("clickers") bibliography. Vanderbilt Center for Teaching website. http://cft.vanderbilt.edu/docs/classroom-response-system-clickers-bibliography/. Updated 2013. Accessed October 25, 2013.

7. UW-Milwaukee Learning Technology Center. Student response systems (SRS)—the UW-system clicker project. http://www4.uwm.edu/ltc/srs/. Updated 2013. Accessed November 20, 2013.

8. Hollister C, Robinson J, Sullivan R. *UBClicks—Resources Relating to the Use of Clickers in Education.* https://docs.google.com/document/d/1afpMCjDU Cfp9e0XaHCn6tyXDG1Wj5MijPOEo1nSfgs0/preview?pli=1#. Updated 2009. Accessed November 20, 2013.

9. Angelo TA, Cross KP. *Classroom Assessment Techniques: A Handbook for College Teachers.* San Francisco, CA: Jossey-Bass Publishers; 1993.

10. Dunaway MK, Orblych MT. Formative assessment: Transforming information literacy instruction. *Ref Serv Rev.* 2011;39(1):24–41.

11. Wang R. The lasting impact of a library credit course. *portal: Libr & Academy.* 2006;6(1):79.

12. Dill E. Do clickers improve library instruction? Lock in your answers now. *J Acad Libr.* 2008;34(6):527–529.

13. Petersohn B. Classroom performance systems, library instruction, and instructional design: A pilot study. *Portal: Lib & Academy.* 2008;8(3):313–324.

14. Buhay D, Best LA, McGuire K. The effectiveness of library instruction: Do student response systems (clickers) enhance learning? *Can J Scholarsh Teach & Learn.* 2010;1(1). http://ir.lib.uwo.ca/cjsotl_rcacea/vol1/iss1/5/.

15. Keough SM. Clickers in the classroom: A review and a replication. *J Manag Educ.* 2012;36(6):822–847. doi:10.1177/1052562912454808.

16. Beatty ID, Gerace WJ, Leonard WJ, Dufresne RJ. Designing effective questions for classroom response system teaching. *Amer J Phys.* 2006;74(1):31–39.

17. Kaneshiro KN, Emmett TW, London SK, et al. Use of an audience response system in an evidence-based mini-curriculum. *Med Ref Serv Q.* 2008;27(3):284–301.

18. Abate LE, Gomes A, Linton A. Engaging students in active learning: Use of a blog and audience response system. *Med Ref Serv Q.* 2011;30(1):12–18.

19. Burkhardt A, Cohen SF. "Turn your cell phones on": Mobile phone polling as a tool for teaching information literacy. *Commun Inform Literacy.* 2012;6(2):191.

20. Hoppenfeld J. Keeping students engaged with web-based polling in the library instruction session. *Libr Hi Tech.* 2012;30(2):235–252. doi: 10.1108/07378831211239933.

21. Mandernach BJ, Hackathorn J. Embracing texting during class. *Teach Professor.* 2010;24(10):1–6.

22. Oakes CE, Demaio DN. "I was able to have a voice without being self-conscious": Students' perceptions of audience response systems in the health sciences curriculum. *J Allied Health.* 2013;42(3):e75–80.

23. Graham CR, Tripp TR, Seawright L, Joeckel, GL. Empowering or compelling reluctant participators using audience response systems. *Active Learn Higher Educ.* 2007;8(3):233–258.

24. Connor E. Perceptions and uses of clicker technology. *J Electron Resour Med Libr.* 2009;6(1):19–32.

25. Pew Internet Project. Device ownership. Pew Research Center website. http://www.pewresearch.org/data-trend/media-and-technology/device-ownership/. Published September 18, 2013. Updated 2013. Accessed March 11, 2014.

26. Sawada D. 3.

27. Ibid.

28. Bloom B. *Taxonomy of Educational Objectives.* New York, NY: David McKay Company, Inc; 1956:196.

29. Bruff D. *Teaching with Classroom Response Systems: Creating Active Learning Environments.* San Francisco, CA: Jossey-Bass; 2009.

30. Connor E. Using cases and clickers in library instruction: Designed for science undergraduates. *Sci & Technol Libr.* 2011;30(3):244–253.

31. Bruff D. 6.

32. Mazur E. *Peer Instruction: A User's Manual.* Upper Saddle River, NJ: Prentice Hall; 1997.

33. Ibid.

34. Bruff D. 29.

35. Bombaro C. Using audience response technology to teach academic integrity. *Ref Serv Rev.* 2007;35(2):296–309.

36. Bruff D. 29.

37. Rimland E. Assessing affective learning using a student response system. *portal: Libr & Academy.* 2013;13(4):385–401.

38. Atkinson C. *The Backchannel: How Audiences Are Using Twitter and Social Media and Changing Presentations Forever.* Berkeley, CA: New Riders; 2009.

39. Angelo TA. 9.

40. Penn State Learning Design Community Hub. Writing effective questions to promote learning. http://ets.tlt.psu.edu/learningdesign/effective_questions. Updated 2010. Accessed January, 2013.

41. Nielsen K, Hansen G, Stav J. Teaching with student response systems (SRS): Teacher-centric aspects that can negatively affect students' experience of using SRS. *Res Learn Technol.* 2013;21.

42. Deleo PA, Eichenholtz S, Sosin AA. Bridging the information literacy gap with "clickers." *J Acad Libr*. 2009;35(5):438–444.

43. Bruff D. 29.

44. Premkumar K, Coupal C. Rules of engagement: 12 tips for successful use of "clickers" in the classroom. *Med Teach*. 2008;30(2):146–149.

45. Caldwell JE. 2.

8

Team-Based Learning

Brandi Tuttle and Adrianne Leonardelli

Team-based learning (TBL) was developed in the 1970s by Dr. Larry Michaelsen, a business professor at the University of Oklahoma, as a way to effectively use teamwork in large classes.[1,2] In recent years, TBL has gained popularity in health sciences education, particularly undergraduate medical education. According to recent estimates, instructors in 77 medical schools in the United States use TBL.[3] As more schools of medicine, nursing, and allied health adopt TBL, medical librarians may be expected to provide instruction using this format. Even if TBL is never fully integrated into the formal educational landscape at your institution, librarians looking for an alternative teaching method may wish to employ TBL principles: think of it as yet another instructional tool for the teaching librarian's toolbox.

WHAT IS TBL?

TBL is an instructional framework that uses active learning and small groups to provide students opportunities to apply newly acquired knowledge resulting in higher-level learning.[4] Although active learning and group work are integral components, TBL is much more than the sum of these parts. TBL requires individual students to come to class having completed an assignment that prepares them for activities in the face-to-face session. The pre-class assignment provides students with the background knowledge needed to complete individual and group quizzes, which are known as Readiness Assessments. After finishing the Readiness Assessments, students work in small teams to complete an activity, or Team Application. The Team Application gives students a chance to apply and build upon content covered in the pre-class assignment. Flipping the traditional instructional model on its head, TBL offers little room for lecture as a majority of class time is devoted to the Team Application. Following the Team Application, students complete peer assessments to rate the preparedness and contributions of fellow group members. The peer assessment is not only an evaluation tool to assist the instructor; it also serves to motivate students and hold them accountable for their actions.

TBL: A STRUCTURED PROCESS

TBL is much more than randomly inserting collaborative or active learning activities into a class session. It follows a very specific, structured process. Whether an instructor is creating an entire curriculum based on TBL, or just one class, the same structure should be used. Instructors should remember the four essential components of TBL as outlined by Michaelson and associates.[5(p10)]

1. Groups must be properly formed *and* managed.
2. Students must be accountable for the quality of their individual *and* group work.
3. Students must have frequent *and* timely feedback.
4. Team assignments must promote both learning *and* team development.

These components can be distilled down to the following steps: Pre-class Assignment, Readiness Assurance Process (i.e., Individual and Group Readiness Assessment Tests), Team Application, and Peer Evaluation (see figure 8.1).

To better understand TBL and how it works, it may help to see it adapted to a library instructional session. Using the following scenario, we will move through the TBL process, providing an overview and relevant examples for each step.

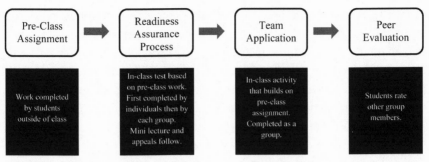

Figure 8.1. The TBL Process

Scenario: Your library has been contacted by a Doctor of Physical Therapy (DPT) Program faculty member who is teaching the Evidence-Based Practice course and requests a session on "Finding the Evidence" for first-year students who are about to enter clinical rotations. The DPT program has recently transitioned from a traditional curriculum to TBL and suggests that the librarian teach the class using this instructional approach.

Pre-class Assignment

Just as it sounds, pre-class work should be completed by individual students outside of the classroom prior to the face-to-face TBL session. These assignments should provide students with the knowledge they will need to successfully complete the Readiness Assessments and Team Application. They should also give students the building blocks necessary for team discussions. If students do not complete pre-class assignments, they will not only do poorly on the Readiness Assessments, but will be ill prepared to participate in team activities in a meaningful way.

Group dynamics play an important role in TBL. Unlike traditional classrooms, students must now answer to their fellow team members, as well as to themselves and the instructor.[6] With a well-formed team, students become accountable to each other and are more motivated to come to class prepared.[7,8] When students are prepared, they are better able to apply knowledge to a real-life scenario and teach their peers. An additional benefit of teams is that "a vast majority . . . can outperform their most knowledgeable member on decision-making tasks."[9(p836)]

Ideally, teams should be created at the beginning of a semester or program and formed strategically based on student strengths, weakness, and personalities by the course instructor or someone very familiar with the students.[10] However, it is our experience that a librarian may be teaching a TBL session to students who have yet to receive team assignments or are not in their regular groups due to scheduling conflicts. Even without previous knowledge of students, the librarian should still make team assignments. At the very least, ask students to count off or draw a number from a hat so that team assignment is somewhat random and less likely to be based on peer cliques.

EXAMPLE DPT PRE-CLASS ASSIGNMENTS FOR "FINDING THE EVIDENCE"

Assign students to

- Watch a video demonstrating how to search PubMed
- Read a journal article about study design and types of research studies
- Complete a hands-on tutorial that allows them to practice their searching skills

Readiness Assurance Process:
Individual and Group Readiness Assessment Tests

The Readiness Assessment Tests (RATs) are used to help gauge student understanding of content covered in the pre-class assignment. The RAT is a brief quiz, usually 10 multiple-choice questions. The quiz should not focus on fact recall, but rather promote discussion and critical thinking.[11] The Individual Readiness Assessment Test (iRAT) is completed independently by each student at the beginning of the face-to-face TBL session. After students complete the iRAT, they work together in teams to complete the same quiz. This is called the Group Readiness Assessment Test (gRAT). The gRAT allows teams to discuss the questions, debate the answers, and teach one another. During the gRAT, each team records their answers on a scratch card, which provides immediate feedback by revealing a star when the correct answer has been chosen (see figure 8.2). Providing students with frequent feedback is critical in TBL as it can improve learning, retention, and team cohesion.[12]

After each team has completed the gRAT, the instructor should discuss the correct answers with the entire class. At this time teams have an opportunity to appeal answers they got wrong. Appeals must be presented

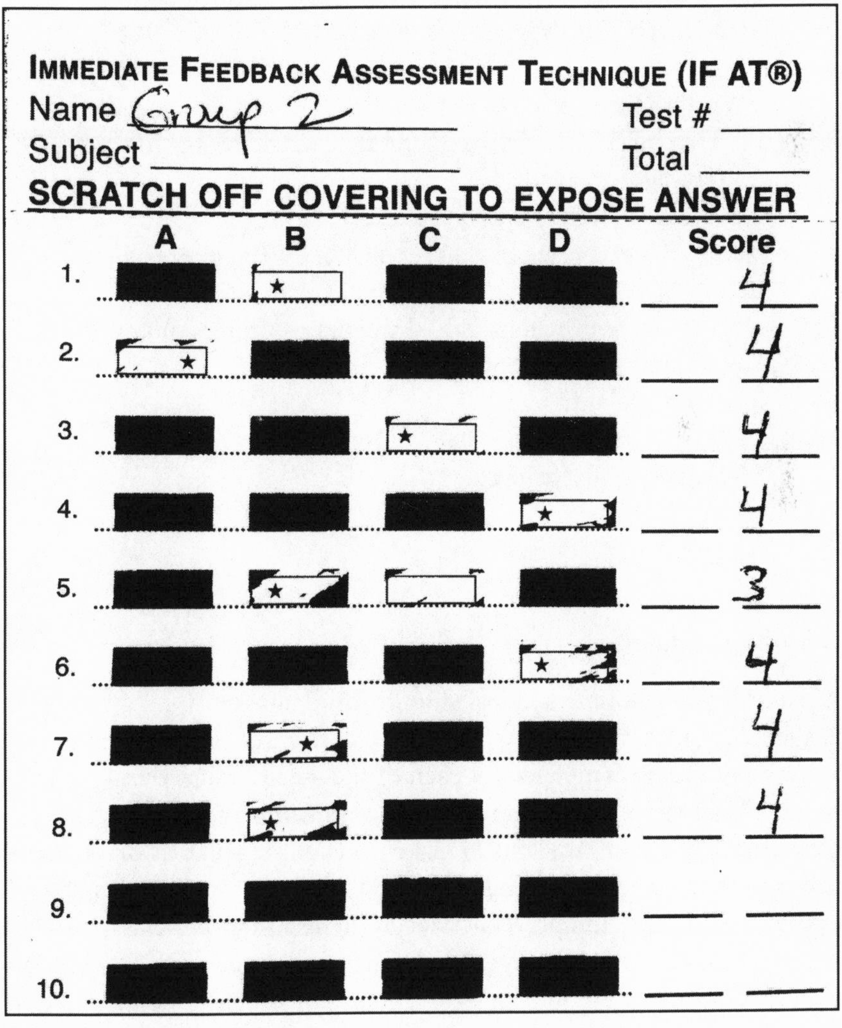

Figure 8.2. TBL Scratch Card

formally, usually written, and based on evidence. During the final step of the Readiness Assurance Process (RAP), instructors provide a very brief and focused lecture to answer questions, clarify content covered in the pre-class assignment, or clear up misconceptions observed during the gRAT.[13]

EXAMPLE DPT READINESS ASSESSMENT TEST QUESTIONS FOR "FINDING THE EVIDENCE"

1. What is the better strategy to find information on potential risks from PTSD, such as depression and dementia, in veterans returning from war?
   a. PTSD *or* veterans *or* dementia
   b. PTSD *and* veterans *and* (dementia *and* depression)
   c. PTSD *and* veterans *and* dementia *or* depression
   d. PTSD *and* veterans *and* (dementia *or* depression)
2. What type of study best answers therapy clinical questions?
   1. Cohort Study
   2. Randomized Controlled Trial
   3. Case-Controlled Study
   4. Case Series

Team Application

A majority of class time is devoted to the third, and most important, step in the TBL process: the Team Application. The Team Application is an assignment that is completed by each of the small groups during a TBL session. When designing Team Applications, instructors should create assignments that require students to make decisions together as this encourages group interaction and engagement.[14,15,16] Team Applications should also allow students to apply knowledge gained from pre-class work in practical and meaningful ways. Michaelsen and associates[17(p47)] describe four distinctive aspects, known as the "four Ss," which guide the creation of the assignment:

1. Assignments should always be designed around a problem that is *significant to students*.
2. All of the students in the class should be working on the *same* problem.
3. Students should be required to make a *specific* choice.
4. Groups should *simultaneously* report their choices.

In addition, Team Applications should be designed in a way that prohibits students from divvying up the work.[18] We recommend distributing assignments piecemeal if necessary (see table 8.1 for an example Team Application).

PEER EVALUATION

At the end of each TBL session, group members complete a Peer Evaluation to provide teammates with constructive feedback and assess their engagement and contributions. This integral step reinforces accountability, a primary tenet of TBL.[19] Qualitative and quantitative feedback provides opportunities to improve group cohesion as well as individual performance. In fact, data from Peer Evaluations are sometimes included as part of a student's grade. Various Peer Evaluation methods are noted in the literature and instructors should experiment to determine which approach is best for their particular setting.[20]

In the authors' DPT class, a Peer Evaluation was completed by students and considered in their overall grade. However, in the one hour TBL session for medical students (outlined in Table 8.1), no grades or Peer Evaluations were administered. Without these important elements, student accountability and engagement were more difficult to attain.

Preferably, instructors will have a block of two to four hours for a TBL class session. However, this amount of time is not always feasible for librarians. In the authors' experience, it is possible to teach a one-hour session using TBL. In such instances, the librarian should take great care to plan the class down to the minute. The outline in table 8.2 offers a structure for how we organized a one-hour TBL session for second-year medical students on finding the best evidence in PubMed.

Table 8.1. Example DPT Team Application: "Finding the Evidence"

Example DPT Team Application: "Finding the Evidence" — Time needed: 3 hours

Case: Your patient, Sam Adams, is a 66 YOM with asthma and osteoarthritis. He has a history of hospitalizations for poor asthma control and is currently taking corticosteroids. He has a total knee replacement scheduled and has been referred to you for preoperative physical therapy. Sam is skeptical about physical therapy before surgery and doesn't see the point. He asks if there is any research that physical therapy can help patients like him.

Identify PICOTT	Patient/ Problem	Intervention	Comparison	Outcome	Type of Question	Type of Study

State the Clinical Question:

Search: Conduct a search in PubMed, CINAHL, and Google Scholar. Use the table below to document your *most successful* search in each of these three resources.

Please provide the following information:
- Search terms (include MeSH and CINAHL headings).
- Documentation of your final search strategy.
- Number of search results retrieved.
- Filters or limits applied.
- Articles: Identify the two best articles from each search.
- Studies: What type of studies did you choose? Why?

Resource Searched	Search Terms / Final Strategy	Number of Results	Filters / Limits	Articles Selected (Give Citations)	Study Type
PubMed					
CINAHL					
Google Scholar					

Table 8.2.   Example of TBL Class Outline for Medical Students: "Finding the Evidence"

Example TBL Class Outline for Medical Students: "Finding the Evidence"	Time needed: 1 hour

Materials needed: Copies of iRAT, gRAT and Team Application, pens or pencils, scratch cards, coins, green/red/yellow cards for voting, computer with overhead (for instructor), one computer for each group

Before Class:
- If necessary, rearrange the classroom to make it conducive for group work.
- Set up an online stopwatch to time RATs and Team Application. Make sure the stopwatch is visible to all students.
- Allow students to sit in their groups (if pre-assigned by their course instructor).

Introductions and Welcome 2 minutes
- Introduce the instructors and purpose of the session.
- Remind students that they completed a pre-work tutorial on study design and searching the literature.

Individual Readiness Assessment Test (iRAT) 5–7 minutes
- Pass the test out to students. Make sure all students have a pen or pencil.
- Allow students five minutes to complete the iRAT.

Group Readiness Assessment Test (gRAT) 5–7 minutes
- If students don't have assigned groups, ask students to count off to form teams.
- Distribute the gRAT, scratch-off cards, and a coin.
- Using the overhead timer, allow groups five minutes to complete the gRAT.
- Float around the classroom to listen but do not provide assistance.

Discussion of gRAT 5–7 minutes
- Review gRAT answers and discuss troublesome questions.
- Clarify misconceptions or confusion overheard as teams worked on the gRAT.

Team Application 20 minutes
- Pass out the Team Application assignment and review the instructions.
- Ask that each group pick a recorder and spokesperson.
- Explain that each group will need to reach a consensus on their answers.

Team Reporting 15 minutes
- Bring the class back together. Ask each team to share their answers.
- Have each team vote simultaneously on their answer to the clinical question using the red, green, or yellow cards (red = no; green = yes; yellow = not sure/not enough evidence).
- Answer student questions and clarify any misconceptions.

Wrap-Up 5–8 minutes
- Have students complete brief peer evaluation forms.
- Summarize class content, highlighting critical points.
- Final questions/comments.
- Collect peer evaluations, iRATs, gRATs, and Team Applications.

BENEFITS AND CHALLENGES
OF TBL IN LIBRARY INSTRUCTION

While there are many advantages to transitioning a course to TBL format, there are also challenges such as faculty and student buy-in. If faculty members provide adequate time and agree to grade a session or course, students are more likely to approach it seriously. Another factor impacting the success of TBL implementation is group formation. Students who have been thoughtfully placed into groups are more likely to work well together and develop into self-managed learning groups.[21(p30)] Working together as a group teaches students how to function in a team environment, increases student accountability and engagement, and ultimately leads to better exam performance.[22,23,24] In addition to the benefits of teamwork and positive group dynamics, TBL focuses less on lecture and allows students to work with newly acquired content, which leads to increased understanding and higher level learning.[25] The immediate feedback provided to students via the RAP and in-class discussions also helps keep students motivated, allows for clarification of key concepts, and enables at-risk students.[26,27]

When teams become dysfunctional, students and the entire TBL process suffer. Students may fail to adequately prepare for class or contribute to the group. The authors have heard many students claim they prefer a lecture-based class over a TBL session. However, it has been our experience that when using TBL, students seem to have a better understanding of core concepts and are better prepared to tackle the Team Application together.

As an instructor, be aware that preparation time for a TBL session may be much greater than a traditional course. In addition, it can be difficult to create good multiple-choice questions based on pre-class assignments that gauge higher order thinking and stimulate discussion. Ensuring that the Team Application is effective and engaging is yet another skill TBL instructors must master. And finally, keep in mind that moving away from *sage on the stage* to *guide on the side* means students will feel empowered to challenge the instructor or content.

CONCLUSION

Ultimately the many benefits of TBL may encourage librarians to adopt this instructional approach. Depending on your faculty, students, time, and space realities, TBL may provide an edge over active learning and lecture-based sessions by motivating students and providing more data on student learning outcomes. At the very least, instruction librarians should be prepared to inform faculty on this style of teaching and offer support and resources as needed.

NOTES

1. Michaelsen LK, Knight AB, Fink LD. *Team-based Learning: A Transformative Use of Small Groups in College Teaching.* 1st ed. Sterling, VA: Stylus Pub.; 2004.

2. Michaelsen LK, Parmelee D, McMahon KK, Levine RE. *Team-Based Learning for Health Professions Education: A Guide to Using Small Groups for Improving Learning.* Sterling, VA: Stylus; 2008.

3. Ibid.

4. Parmelee D, Michaelsen LK, Cook S, Hudes PD. Team-based learning: A practical guide. AMEE guide no. 65. *Med Teach.* 2012;34(5):e275–287.

5. Michaelsen LK. 2.

6. Michaelsen LK, Sweet M. The essential elements of team-based learning. *New Dir Teach & Learn.* 2008:2008(116):7–27.

7. Michaelsen LK. 1.

8. Michaelsen LK. 2.

9. Michaelsen LK, Watson WE, Black RH. A realistic test of individual versus group consensus decision making. *J Appl Psychol.* 1989;74(5):834–839.

10. Michaelsen LK. 2.

11. Ibid.

12. Michaelsen LK. 6.

13. Parmelee DX, Michaelsen LK. Twelve tips for doing effective team-based learning (TBL). *Med Teach.* 2010;32(2):118–122.

14. Michaelsen LK. 1.

15. Michaelsen LK. 2.

16. Michaelsen LK. 6.

17. Michaelsen LK. 2.

18. Michaelsen LK. 6.

19. Michaelsen LK. 2.

20. Ibid.

21. Michaelsen LK, Watson WE, Black RH. A realistic test of individual versus group consensus decision making. *J Appl Psychol* 1989;74(5):834–839.

22. Michaelsen LK. 6.

23. Koles PG, Stolfi A, Borges NJ, Nelson S, Parmelee DX. The impact of team-based learning on medical students' academic performance. *Acad Med.* Nov 2010;85(11):1739–1745.

24. Sisk RJ. Team-based learning: Systematic research review. *J Nurs Educ.* Dec 2011;50(12):665–669.

25. Michaelsen LK. 2.

26. Ibid

27. Michaelsen LK. 6.

ADDITIONAL READINGS

Jacobson TE. Team-based learning in an information literacy course. *Communications in Information Literacy.* 2012;5(2):82–101.

Mennenga HA, Smyer T. A model for easily incorporating team-based learning into nursing education. *Int J Nurs Educ Scholarsh.* 2010;(7)Article4.

Metcalf S. Will team-based learning mesh well with library instruction? *LOEX Quarterly.* 2006;33(3).

Michaelsen LK, Sweet M. The essential elements of team-based learning. *New Directions for Teaching and Learning.* 2008(116):7–27.

Parmelee DX. Team-based learning: moving forward in curriculum innovation: A commentary. *Med Teach.* 2010;32(2):105–107.

Parmelee DX, Michaelsen LK. Twelve tips for doing effective Team-Based Learning (TBL). *Med Teach.* 2010;32(2):118–122.

Thomas PA, Bowen CW. A controlled trial of team-based learning in an ambulatory medicine clerkship for medical students. *Teach Learn Med.* Jan 2011;23(1):31–36.

Thompson BM, Schneider VF, Haidet P, et al. Team-based learning at ten medical schools: Two years later. *Med Educ.* Mar 2007;41(3):250–257.

Thompson BM, Schneider VF, Haidet P, Perkowski LC, Richards BF. Factors influencing implementation of team-based learning in health sciences education. *Acad Med.* Oct 2007;82(10 Suppl):S53–56.

WEBSITE

Team-Based Learning Collaborative http://www.teambasedlearning.org/

9

Lesson Study in the Nursing Curriculum

Bryan S. Vogh, Hans Kishel, and Eric Jennings

At the University of Wisconsin–Eau Claire three members of the undergraduate nursing program saw a need to strengthen evidence-based practice (EBP) and information literacy skills within their courses. An interdisciplinary team of library and nursing faculty were assembled to address this problem. Lesson study was selected to address the problem because of facilitator expertise, experience using lesson study by library faculty, and the lack of evidence in the literature of the use of lesson study in a nursing environment. The flexibility, evaluative methods, and ease of using the lesson study methodology were identified as traits that seemed to make it well suited to create lessons that would increase information literacy and EBP skills in the nursing curriculum. This chapter will focus on lesson study and how it was implemented, and advises readers on using lesson study to introduce and enhance information literacy across an undergraduate nursing curriculum.

WHAT IS LESSON STUDY AND WHY WAS IT SELECTED?

Lesson study is a teaching improvement process wherein a group of educators works collaboratively to plan, teach, observe, and evaluate an individual lesson with a shared goal of increasing engagement and learning by students as evidenced by the goals and objectives that the educators collectively create. Lesson study began in Japanese elementary schools, but has since expanded into higher education in the United States. For a more detailed look at the lesson study process see Lewis's *Lesson Study: A Handbook of Teacher-Led Instructional Change* (2002) or Cerbin's *Lesson Study: Using Classroom Inquiry to Improve Teaching and Learning in Higher Education* (2011).

Lesson study is a methodology for a team of educators to create, assess, and revise a single lesson to maximize student learning. It is a cyclical process that can be repeated as many times as needed. First, the team of educators reads relevant literature about the methodology of lesson study and discipline-specific pedagogical methods. Based on the readings and course objective(s), the team identifies one or more goals. Second, the team designs the lesson. Third, one member from the team teaches the lesson and other team members take notes while observing the students. The observations are learner focused and are targeted at evaluating the effectiveness of the planned lesson based on student engagement and understanding. Additional data on the effectiveness of the lesson can be gathered through a variety of assessment methods such as surveys and focus groups. Fourth, the team, including the instructor, reviews all evaluative material and discusses the findings. Fifth, based on the findings, the team revises (if needed) the original lesson to improve engagement and understanding. At this point, the lesson study process can be repeated.

See table 9.1 (adapted from Stombaugh A, Sperstad R, Vanwormer A, Jennings E, Kishel H, Vogh B., 2013] for definitions of each step and an estimated number of meetings for each step.

FIRST STEPS

What we did: Because of previous experience with lesson study, two librarians and a facilitator explained lesson study to the uninitiated team members. At this first meeting, nursing faculty and librarians discussed the information literacy problems they had encountered. Teaching approaches were discussed and time was spent examining lesson study methodology. Sharing successes from prior lesson studies on campus was an integral part of this introductory meeting. At the end of the meeting, team members agreed to bring lists of concerns about student work that could be used as part of a discussion to shape goals.

Table 9.1. **Lesson Study Steps and Definitions**

Lesson Study Steps	Definition	Estimated Number of Meetings (45–90 min.)
Identify goals of lesson study	Team reviews and discusses literature, identifies needs for class, and defines goals of specific lesson to be taught.	1–3
Plan the lesson	Team plans a single lesson based upon identified goals.	3–6
Teach and observe the lesson	Member(s) of group teach lesson. Other members observe students in class.	1
Discuss findings from the lesson	Team meets to discuss data collected during entire process (focus group questions, observations of students).	1
Revise the lesson	Based upon the discussion, group may choose to adjust the lesson and run the lessons study process again.	1–2

Advice: Before starting a lesson study process, familiarize yourself with the lesson study research. Be prepared to share examples that have used this methodology successfully and discuss its use on your campus. Schedule regular meetings with your team; start meeting at least one semester before the first lesson takes place so that you give your team enough time to prepare. Before the team sets goals members should review the curriculum to identify a specific course(s) that would benefit most from using the lesson study methodology.

SHARED GOAL SETTING

What we did: Our team initially identified two overlapping goals for the lesson. These goals were improving information literacy skills (library) and integrating EBP across the nursing curriculum (nursing). Through a series of meetings, the team came up with a unified goal for the lesson study: students will be able to retrieve various levels of scholarly information and evaluate their usefulness to clinical practice demonstrating development of skill in EBP. In order to meet this goal, the team decided to implement multiple lessons, each of which had its own goal and would be scaffolded in a sequential manner for students as they progressed through the nursing curriculum.

Advice: Proposed goals should be generated outside of the team meetings with the time at the meetings reserved to share, refine, and discuss ideas to take advantage of the face-to-face time with all team members. It is imperative for all team members to have a shared understanding of the terminology used in each discipline and how it relates to the students' learning. Time spent on goal setting pays off in benefits later in the process especially if you decide to use a scaffolded approach to integrating library instruction across the curriculum.

DEVELOPING THE LESSON

What we did: The team met and identified a librarian who would teach the lesson. We then developed exercises for the worksheet that maximized student participation and engagement. Nursing and library faculty contributed examples that were tailored to demonstrate key concepts covered in the lesson. Specific resources and exercises were included in order to build a base level of skill. Subsequent lessons built on those skills to reinforce prior learning and continue building information literacy skills and knowledge. Worksheets were designed to facilitate group work and to provide students with a structured path through the lesson and the group work. Worksheet questions were designed to highlight the information literacy concepts. The entire class participated in a discussion at the end of each lesson.

Advice: The class discussion and group work are just as important as exposing the learners to the information resources because the questions reinforce the information literacy concepts being practiced. Worksheet development is vital as this content guides the students toward the goal of the lesson.

TEACHING THE LESSON

What we did: In general the lessons were composed of the following parts: introductory lecture, demonstration, group exercises, and class discussion. For details on the specific lessons we created and taught, see

our article in *Nurse Educator* or go to http://libguides.uwec.edu/content.
php?pid=330537&sid=2703682.

Advice: In an introduction of no more than five minutes, provide an
outline that includes how much time for each item in the lesson to set student expectations. Use a digital timer to keep things on track and prompt
students when they should be half-way through an exercise. The library
home page should serve as the launch pad for your demonstration(s) so
that students can replicate the search process outside of class.

OBSERVING THE LESSON

What we did: All team members not teaching the lesson acted as observers. Questions and points of interest were generated by the team before-
hand to help structure the observations related to student learning. When
observing the lesson team members were distributed throughout the room
and recorded student engagement and participation.

Advice: Develop a checklist of points of observation related to student
learning. Make sure that team members can observe the majority of students, and tell observers that they should feel free to move around the
room. Adding peers as observers allows others to see the lesson and will
provide valuable insight from a non-team member perspective.

EVALUATING THE LESSON

What we did: We held focus groups after each lesson. Focus group questions challenged the students to articulate the purpose of the lesson and
give feedback on the usefulness of the worksheet.

Advice: Focus group facilitator(s) should not be the course instructor or
the team member who conducted the lesson.

DISCUSSING AND REVISING THE LESSON

What we did: One week after each lesson was taught team members met to
discuss the observation notes and student responses to focus group questions.

Team members discussed themes that emerged from the data. Based upon the results of this discussion, the team decided whether the lesson study had achieved the defined goal and if the lesson needed refinement.

Advice: Make sure to schedule a wrap-up meeting as soon as possible after the lesson is taught and allow adequate time for reflection on whether goals and course objectives were met. In the same meeting or a separate one, discuss any changes to increase engagement and analyze comments from the students. Revisions to the lesson should reflect an attempt to enhance student learning. You will inevitably find something to change in your lesson. Work on the next iteration of the lesson, including the worksheet, while the lesson is fresh in your mind.

CONCLUSION

Lesson study is an effective way to design library instruction that integrates information literacy into a course. Our team has successfully used lesson study to scaffold information literacy into four classes within the nursing curriculum. This collaboration has improved the relationship between the faculty in both departments and resulted in a dialogue about wider inclusion of information literacy and EBP in the evolving nursing curriculum. Lesson study can be used to create strong relationships for future collaborations while focusing on creating outcome-based student-focused learning experiences.

For further information including lesson outlines, worksheets, and handouts, see http://libguides.uwec.edu/content.php?pid=330537&sid= 2703682 or contact the authors.

FURTHER READING

Cerbin B. *Lesson Study: Using Classroom Inquiry to Improve Teaching and Learning in Higher Education.* Sterling, VA: Stylus; 2011.

Lewis C. *Lesson Study: A Handbook of Teacher-led Instructional Change.* Philadelphia, PA: Research for Better Schools, Inc.; 2012.

Stombaugh A, Sperstad R, Vanwormer A, Jennings E, Kishel H, Vogh B. Using lesson study to integrate information literacy throughout the curriculum. *Nurse Educ.* 2013;38(4):173–177.

IV

INSTRUCTIONAL MODES AND ASSESSMENT

10

Online Instruction

Megan B. Inman

Course content in the higher education environment is delivered through a variety of methods. Courses are frequently designated as one of four types of instruction.[1] The first is known as a traditional or face-to-face instruction. This is where no content is hosted in an online format. Another type is a web-facilitated class in which a course management system might be used only for uploading assignments and syllabi but much of the content remains in a face-to-face setting. The third—known as a hybrid, or blended, course—combines both in-person instruction and online content. Finally, there is the fully online course where most or all of the course material is provided online.

At this time, distance education and online instruction are almost synonymous. However, distance education first began with independent study courses in which students were provided with some form of media such as radio, television, or audiocassettes.[2] The creation of the Internet forever changed distance education, and just like all formats of technology, online instruction is rapidly growing and expanding. A 2013 survey of online learning in higher education found that there are over 6.7 million higher education students taking at least one course online.[3]

There are many benefits with online instruction. It provides more students with access to education, often by eliminating issues that are frequently associated with time and location.[4] In addition, students have the opportunity to learn materials at a pace that is the most suitable for them.[5] Institutions also reap the benefits of online instruction, and the lower cost in providing students with a worthy education is a very attractive incentive for postsecondary institutions.[6]

As universities are competing for enrollment of both of undergraduate and graduate students, the demographic of online students is rapidly changing.[7] With technology frequently changing, it takes a different type of student to succeed in an online environment. Students must have a high level of motivation and a high level of self-direction.[8] This is at times due to the fact that the occasional passive classroom has now become an active learning environment.[9] The change in learning environment and necessity for basic technology skills might also be a challenge for some adult learners. In addition to students needing different study and technology skills, it also requires instructors to change the way they design course materials. This chapter is designed to review the major concepts within online instruction and incorporate how librarians can become involved with online instruction.

ONLINE INSTRUCTION TIPS AND TECHNIQUES

A common misconception regarding creating online courses is that one can simply transfer the materials used in face-to-face teaching into an online format.[10] Although this can and is often done, it is not the best way to connect with distance education students. The course content should be manipulated into a format that will best help students connect with the information online.

In fact, oftentimes, a new mind-set is needed when approaching online instruction. New strategies are essential in the areas of planning, class creation, and participant interaction.[11] To start with, faculty and students must have access to some form of technical support.[12] In addition, a basic course or workshop is a great way to build background knowledge and technology skills. Having a solid base knowledge of technical aspects can help both students and faculty feel at ease when using course software.

Often universities will encourage distance education students to pursue basic technology courses that cover a range of topics, from attaching documents in e-mails to navigating course management systems (CMSs). Faculty members often find it beneficial to create tutorials for their students that will assist them in developing the knowledge needed to navigate their particular CMSs and the course content that they have produced. This tutorial could be a video tutorial or a set of written instructions. Some instructors find it useful to create a quick first assignment or quiz over the CMS as well as the syllabus to be sure students are familiar with the CMS and the course expectations.

In regard to instructors, training during faculty orientation will help to bridge any gaps in the use of these types of systems. A good background in the institution's CMS will ideally aid the stigma where faculty find it more time-consuming to teach an online course than the traditional format.[13] One idea is to create a forum where faulty can come together and offer suggestions and support with their online teaching. A wonderful option would be to host this forum at the library. Furthermore, the library could partner with the university's office of faculty education to help faculty become familiar with library resources and services that are offered.

In the creation of online instruction materials it is essential to understand the background of the learners or users. People often think of online learners as working adults; however, this is not always the case.[14] In higher education, the population can consist of a large age range with varying technology and computer skills. As with any mode of instruction, the content provided within courses needs to meet the requirements of the students. Faculty teaching in this environment must work diligently to engage learners and keep the student population interested in course content. Instructors need to clearly communicate expectations with their students. It is also recommended that faculty set up a minimum length of time in which they will respond to student questions.[15]

DESIGNING ONLINE COURSES AND MODULES

Many librarians are moving beyond insertion into a faculty's course by offering semester-long courses for credit. LaGuardia Community College offered such courses where the content included searching strategies and evaluation.[16] Students were required to conduct mini research projects and expected to explain how they found information and whether or not it was appropriate for course use. Although the creation of a semester-long course for credit can be tedious, it is well worth the time spent.

Planning online courses is more involved than taking the traditional class session and converting it into an online format. Online course design should include a multitude of ways to become engrossed in the content for students, such as the following:[17]

- A variety of learning activities (done both synchronously and asynchronously)
- Video lectures
- Varied website activities
- Interaction through discussion boards, virtual classrooms, and webcams

Online instruction can be further improved by combining the use of asynchronous CMSs, for instance, Blackboard or Moodle, with a synchronous lecture or meeting instrument like Saba.[18] Using a meeting tool aids in creating an active learning experience where students must participate in class as well as create a collaborative space. This type of combination helps to create a more traditional classroom environment.

The creation of noncourse discussion boards is a great way to encourage the sense of community that is sometimes lacking in the online instruction environment. Within a CMS there are a variety of methods to enhance the online experience for students, such as[19]

- Creating an area where students can post biographical information about themselves
- Posting frequently asked questions and issues board
- Encouraging entire class discussions on noncourse topics
- Promoting student-driven discussion with small groups
- Having an open forum where students can read and critique assignments

Online tutorials can be used to cover a variety of concepts without requiring students to view an entire lecture session. This could allow for more engagement with the student. Online tutorials are often best designed by using modules as opposed to an entire class session on a topic. Modules are a mini session on a topic that is often a part of a much larger instruction session,[20] and are often created because information is easier to absorb for students when broken down into smaller components. A library class on searching for *evidence-based medicine* could contain the following modules:

- An introduction to evidence-based medicine
- Types of studies and levels of evidence
- Searching for evidence-based materials in CINAHL (Cumulative Index to Nursing and Allied Health Literature)
- Searching for evidence-based articles in MEDLINE via PubMed
- Searching for evidence-based articles in MEDLINE via Ovid
- Effectively using the evidence-based medicine reviews database

In the modules, it is important to clearly state your educational objectives and purpose in creating the tutorial. Try using interactive no-risk quizzes that would encourage students to participate in the recorded tutorial. These quizzes can be as simple as a one-question multiple-choice slide inserted into the module on a major topic tutorial.

A portion of online course design planning should be designated for course assessments. Assessment is an important aspect of all courses, particularly in the case of online instruction. It can be difficult to gauge student reactions without visual cues. However, there are multitudes of options that can be used. Online assessment techniques can include[21]

- Peer evaluations
- Graded discussion boards
- Rubrics
- Graded chats
- Timed quizzes/tests
- Self-assessments
- Portfolios
- Recorded group presentations

CMSs permit easy insertion of assessments. If possible, librarians can suggest to faculty the option of supplying students with a pretest and posttest measurement. The assessments could be supplied around an assignment.

LIBRARIAN INVOLVEMENT IN AN EXISTING ONLINE COURSE

Many times faculty do not have time in their syllabus for a library orientation or class. Libraries can offer their support to instructors of distance education with library materials. This can easily be done by creating library tutorials or handouts that can then be placed in to an online course.

Librarians have the unique opportunity to provide users with information at their point of need. One unique opportunity for providing online instruction is through embedding librarians within a CMS. Through CMSs such as Moodle and Blackboard, librarians can gain access to an area which the student accesses daily.

It has been shown that "students benefit from asynchronous [library] instruction materials."[22] The idea of an embedded librarian began to appear in the literature in 2004.[23] It started with the use of tutorial modules that faculty could include in their online courses. Inserting librarians, in addition to their content, was the following step. This opportunity allowed for librarians to ensure that students were able to access information from a distance and without having to step into a library.

There are many different ways of becoming involved within a CMS. One method is to embed yourself in a semester-long course. This is best initiated by forming a close relationship with a faculty member and offering to insert library resources within his or her course. A clear line of communication is a basic requirement in working in a faculty's CMS. You will need to closely work together to determine what content needs to be included or is desired by the faculty member within the course.

When it comes time to add the course content, your faculty member will need to add the librarian as some sort of teaching assistant or a course builder. Often the differences between levels of course access will grant the user grade book access. Other options include providing the content to the faculty member you are working with and then having him or her place the information in the course.

Content within the CMS can cover a broad spectrum. Often library handouts or videos are uploaded to the course. These can cover specific databases related to the course or more general orientation type of material. A helpful feature of CMSs is that the content within courses can be "dumped" into additional classes or, rather, copied over from semester to semester. This saves a great deal of time when creating content for CMSs.

Discussion boards are a great place for librarians to get involved as well. The discussion board serves as a place where students can ruminate on instruction as well as a method for instructors and librarians to monitor progress of students.[24] A forum could be created in which the librarian can monitor a board for any question related to the library, such as database searching or proper citation methods. Daily monitoring could become tedious, particularly if the librarian is embedded in multiple courses. It would be advised to set virtual hours or clearly communicate that the board will be checked for questions three times a week for instance.

Faculty can be advised to create a folder of library information where the librarian can then insert library tools and resources. If the library utilizes a feature such as LibGuides, this can be placed or linked into a CMS as well. The idea of using a folder is a great idea for courses that have a final term paper. Some of the resources that can be contained in a library resources folder include links to relevant course databases, step-by-step instruction handouts, library orientation videos, and helpful web resources.

CMSs offer additional features to enhance the instructor experience. One very beneficial component of CMSs for librarians includes statistics. Many CMSs allow for statistics tracking of inserted resources. This feature is particularly helpful for faculty to see if students are appropriately using library resources.

CONCLUSION

Online education in colleges and universities is expanding at a feverish rate and with this type of growth comes new opportunities for librarians to work with faculty to move beyond the traditional instruction session. As mentioned earlier, time is less of a factor when it comes to scheduling a library session. Modules, help sheets, tutorials, and discussion boards can be seamlessly added into the CMS. Online statistics features can provide insight into student habits that would not be possible in the face-to-face environment. Furthermore, many CMSs come with built-in quizzing features that can be used to test for information retention. Best of all, online instruction means that librarians can work with faculty to connect students with library information at their point of need within their CMSs.

NOTES

1. Bolliger DU, Erichsen EA. Student satisfaction with blended and online courses based on personality type. *Can J Learn & Technol.* 2013;39(1): 1–23.

2. Ibid.

3. Allen IE, Seaman J. *Changing Course: Ten Years of Tracking Online Education in the United States.* Babson Survey Research Group and Quahog Research Group, LLC; 2013: http://sloanconsortium.org/node/384451. Accessed February 27, 2014.

4. Crawford-Ferre HG, Wiest LR. Effective online instruction in higher education. *Q Rev of Distance Educ.* 2012;13(1):11.

5. Bollinger DU. 1.

6. Garbett C. Activity-based costing models for alternative modes of delivering on-line courses. *Eur J Open, Distance & E-Learning.* 2011(1):1–14.

7. Mayes R, Luebeck J, Ku H, Akarasriworn C, Korkmaz Ö. Themes and strategies for transformative online instruction: A review of literature and practice. *Q Rev of Distance Educ.* 2011;12(3):151.

8. Parker A. Identifying predictors of academic persistence in distance education. *Usdla J.* 2003;17(1):55–62.

9. Mayes R. 7.

10. Koontz FR, Li H, Compora DP. *Designing Effective Online Instruction: A Handbook for Web-Based Courses.* Lanham, MD: Rowman & Littlefield Education; 2006.

11. Crawford-Ferre HG. 4.

12. Osman ME. Students' reaction to WebCT: Implications for designing on-line learning environments. *Int J Instr Media.* 2005;32(4):353–362.

13. Gabriel MA, Kaufield KJ. Reciprocal mentorship: An effective support for online instructors. *Mentoring & Tutoring: Partnership in Learn.* 2008;16(3):311–327.

14. Koontz FR. 10.

15. Sunderland J. New communication practices, identity and the psychological gap: The affective function of e-mail on a distance doctoral programme. *Stud High Educ.* 2002;27(2):233–246.

16. Ovadia S, White S. Bringing an online credit research class from concept to reality. *J Lib and Inform Serv Distance Learn.* 2010;4(4):197–207.

17. Crawford-Ferre HG. 4.

18. Mayes R. 7.

19. Ibid.

20. Koontz FR. 10.

21. Gaytan J, McEwen BC. Effective online instructional and assessment strategies. *Amer J Distance Educ.* 2007;21(3):117–132.

22. Henrich KJ, Attebury RI. Using blackboard to assess course-specific asynchronous library instruction. *Internet Ref Serv Q.* 2013;17(3–4):167–179.

23. Clark S, Chinburg S. Research performance in undergraduates receiving face-to-face versus online library instruction: A citation analysis. *J Libr Admin.* 2010;50(5–6):530–542.

24. Osman ME. 12.

11

Face-to-Face Instruction

Michele Malloy and Sarah Cantrell

Face-to-face instruction is typically in person and constitutes an environment where learning happens in real time, synchronously. The format of face-to-face instruction can vary, from one-shot or stand-alone group sessions, to guest lectures, to fully developed courses spanning several days to an entire semester or year within the curriculum.

At the heart of a good, in-person library instruction session is a skilled teacher, a role that takes ongoing effort, commitment, and patience. Parker Palmer states that "good teaching cannot be reduced to technique; good teaching comes from the identity and integrity of the teacher."[1(p15)] He elaborates by explaining that good teachers have an ability to make connections between themselves, their subjects, and their students—that they are weavers. We can make personal connections with our learners, engaging them in conversation as they enter the class, for example, and showing genuine interest in their day-to-day activities. During our instruction sessions, we can try to make the subject matter as relatable as possible to events in their lives, whether it's an upcoming assignment or something that will impact patient care.

Crafting a good environment in which students can learn is ideal. In his 2004 article "What makes great teachers great?" Ken Bain suggests that there are several principles that good teachers seem to include in their sessions, such as creating a natural critical learning environment, incorporating an interdisciplinary approach, and not simply giving students answers. These good teachers, Bain argues, "get students' attention and keep it" by using techniques like case-based scenarios, and they "create diverse learning experiences."[2(pB8)]

Face-to-face library instruction sessions also feature several key elements. Nancy H. Dewald identifies several practical characteristics of good library instruction: ensuring that library instruction is course related and assignment driven, includes active learning and opportunities for collaboration, is both auditory and visual, provides clear learning objectives, teaches concepts and not just the how-to, and finally keeps the door open for learners to follow up with the librarian in the future.[3] These characteristics match up with Chickering and Gamson's "Seven Principles for Good Practice in Undergraduate Education,"[4] which suggest that good practice uses active learning techniques, gives prompt feedback, emphasizes time on task, and communicates high expectations, among others.

LESSON PLANNING

Having a well-laid-out lesson plan that matches the learner's needs is key, not only for face-to-face instruction, but also for all instruction endeavors. A well-developed plan will address those very elements that both Dewald and Chickering and Gamson[5,6] raise: setting up objectives, including opportunities for active learning; teaching concepts rather than basic how-to demonstrations; communicating high expectations; and so forth. During the planning process, you should determine the lesson topics and identify what you hope for learners to gain by the end of the session.

There are numerous design models for lesson planning, which feature many similar characteristics. Heinich, Molenda, Russell, and Smaldino[7] refer to the ABCDs of writing objectives wherein one begins by naming the Audience for whom the objective is intended, the Behavior or skill to be demonstrated, the Conditions under which this skill will be observed, and the Degree to which the new skill must be mastered and thereby assessed.

In *Understanding by Design*, Wiggins and McTighe present the Backward Design model.[8] The three stages of this design model involve (1) identifying your desired results (i.e., the learning objectives and what the learners should be able to do by the end of the session), (2) determining acceptable evidence (i.e., how will you know that students have achieved or arrived at the desired results), and (3) planning learning experiences and instruction (i.e., what knowledge, skills, and activities will help you achieve the desired results). The authors indicate that teachers must think about assessment before deciding what and how they will teach, which initially might be challenging for instructors, but ultimately constitutes a best practice.

Booth presents the USER instructional design method in *Reflective Teaching, Effective Learning: Instructional Literacy for Library Educators*.[9] In the Understand phase, one should start by identifying the problem that instruction can solve. The Structure phase defines what participants should be able to accomplish, first by "creating targets—goals, objectives, and outcomes" and then by identifying methods to "involve learners using delivery techniques, technologies, and activities."[10(pp95–96)] Third, the Engage phase involves creating the instruction products, developing materials, and delivering the instruction. And finally, the Reflect phase asks the instructor to assess the impact of instruction.

In order to appeal to multiple learning styles, a mix of didactic and active learning is key, as small-group work or comparable activities may not appeal to all learners. Throughout the face-to-face session, it's advantageous to give them preliminary instructions about what is going to happen and why.

Once you have a plan in place, it's time to consider execution. The "Introduction to Instructional Techniques" chapter in this volume introduced foundational concepts that aid teachers in development and preparation, and many other helpful sources exist to continue building these skills.[11,12] The following tailored tips will specifically enhance in-person curriculum-integrated teaching and allow you to move beyond the basics and enjoy interacting with your class.

ACCEPT UNCERTAINTY

When teaching in front of a live class, things simply won't always go exactly as planned. Sometimes this creates problems, but ultimately a strong instructor can employ uncertainty to improve the classroom experience. Unplanned mishaps involving technology, timing, and student attendance or preparation require adaptability. Anticipate potential issues and be ready with contingency plans. For example, if a technology failure limits display of slides, rely on handouts and white boards. Instructors also need to recognize their own mistakes and uncertainty. When faced with personal mistakes, either admit to the mistakes and correct competently, or use the error as a teaching opportunity, demonstrating an issue students may also face. This can be especially effective when teaching searching techniques. Respond to a weak search or error with, "So, what can we do if this happens? How can we fix it?"; listen to the suggestions of your learners; and then demonstrate.

Be comfortable with temporary silence. Teachers would prefer that students immediately answer every question, but they need time to think and respond. If a student asks a question the instructor isn't able to answer, this presents a chance to problem solve as a group by asking students for input, showing potential sources, and if needed offering to follow up after class.

LET YOURSELF PERFORM

As mentioned in an earlier chapter, performance is a recognized aspect of teaching,[13] but this doesn't discount the preparation and skill needed to appear effortless. Practice for an instructional session, not simply by reading a script or performing rote actions, but by using mirrors, recordings, and colleagues as an initial audience so you'll be able to gauge reactions. Observe other skilled performers, librarians and faculty members in all disciplines, as well as speakers, actors, or comedians in any field. Identify how they capture the audience's interest and modify these methods to match your teaching style. Start simply with eye contact, expressive delivery, and gestures. Demonstrate genuine enthusiasm; students recognize and rise to match a teacher's interest level, especially if the passion is paired with practical examples. Like any entertainer, an instructor requires feedback. Appeal to the "audience" by obviously welcoming interaction, laughter, questions, and constructive input.

MAKE STUDENTS THE FOCUS

Though this tip may initially seem obvious, it can be easy to focus overly on the content or process and fail to truly perceive and involve our learners. When teaching within the curriculum, knowing your population is essential. Become aware of the full curriculum, taking into account concurrent and previous courses so you're able to use those content examples for practical appeal. Acknowledge and plan for diversity of students' interests and background experiences. Directly engage your class, both as a whole unit and individually.[14] Cultivate "plants" by identifying and addressing students you already know or by approaching participants during embedded group activities to solicit their help, "That's a perfect example. Would you mind sharing it with the class during the discussion?" As you teach, notice student reactions and tailor your class as you go, not only in the moment by elaborating on or shortening certain sections but also later when revising the curriculum. In order to encourage reflective lifelong learning and demonstrate curricular integration, always tie instruction back to how and when students will use new skills and knowledge.[15]

CREATE A SUPPORTIVE CLASSROOM CLIMATE

Together, instructors and learners create a classroom climate, or "the intellectual, social, emotional, and physical environments in which our students learn."[16] Improving this learning environment can have an exponential impact on both attitudes and educational retention. Keep track of the overall class dynamic, and ensure that students are supporting each other rather than providing negative feedback. Since instructional components involving the library tend to focus on skills rather than memorization, these classes can easily stress the goal of improving methods rather than identifying incorrect choices. During class, respond to weaker responses with patience, clear explanations, positive alternatives, and no judgmental attitude. Encourage all questions and demonstrate accessibility both in and outside the classroom. By modeling and praising supportive behaviors, instructors create a productive and respectful learning atmosphere.

USE THE PHYSICAL SPACE

Whether you are teaching a small or large group, the actual classroom strongly impacts how your students perceive and participate in face-to-face sessions. Visit the classroom before teaching, even if you have been there before, and assess the layout and resources. In smaller settings, take charge of your space and move tables, chairs, and equipment to best match your goals. Larger rooms can be harder to manage, but make sure you aren't tied to a podium or stage; feel free to move around even the largest lecture halls by requesting a clip-on microphone. Even when using a slide presentation, supplement with handouts, props, whiteboards, and visual aids. During the class, walk around and embed smaller group activities[17] to reinforce teaching and allow for student movement.

TAKE CONTROLLED RISKS: ENHANCE AND INNOVATE

Participating in curriculum-integrated instruction becomes increasingly comfortable and predictable when you work at an institution for an extended period of time. Facilitate the growth of the curriculum and your own teaching skills by continually revising your methods and adding more student-centered and reflective elements. In order to control risky new techniques, roll out only one or two new ideas during each session. Stay informed by reading about educational techniques, participating in instructional development sessions, and communicating with colleagues. To start, employ embedded group work, case-based activities, panels, and student role-play scenarios. Integrate technological supplements such as student response systems (clickers), preparatory web-based tutorials, and Smart Boards. Next, investigate instructional methods such as PBL (problem-based learning), team-based learning, the flipped classroom, concept mapping, contextualization, and interprofessional education.[18,19] When implementing new methods, be forgiving of yourself and realize that not all innovations work with every course and population; don't assume that you did something wrong or that the technique isn't useful, just notice potential limitations and adapt.

ASSESS AND IMPROVE

A later chapter on assessment will present methods of evaluating curriculum by targeting both students and instructors. As you plan your lesson, think about how you will know when the students have achieved the desired objectives. During in-person sessions, this could be as simple as a One-Minute Paper or a Muddiest Point exercise, or lead to a more in-depth quiz or research paper.

Continually assessing yourself as an instructor is also essential to development of expertise and confidence. Ask for student and peer feedback. Allow other librarians to observe your instruction sessions. Certainly, there is an element of personal fear in asking for this type of input, but it can truly allow you to grow as a teacher.

CONCLUSION

Becoming a good face-to-face instructor takes dedication and practice. Think of the best teachers you have had and reflect upon what it was about them that made them so good. Did he listen to you with undivided attention? Was she so enthusiastic about the subject matter that she made even the most boring of topics incredibly fascinating? Good teachers have thought about their lesson plans, giving full consideration to what they want the learners to achieve by the end of the session. They have selected activities that support this learning and considered how they will assess the students' learning and their own impact as teachers.

Face-to-face instruction requires that you accept a certain element of uncertainty, and asks that you allow yourself to perform. Making the students the focus can go a long way and contribute to creating a supportive classroom environment. In-person courses allow instructors to use physical space to engage and relate to students, so take advantage of the situation and retain the attention of participants by moving around and adding props. Continue to develop educational skills by researching and trying new techniques. Through integration of these tips, librarians can become essentially intertwined with the curriculum and our worth can be even more appreciated by students and faculty.

NOTES

1. Palmer PJ. The heart of a teacher. *Change*. 1997;29(6):14–21.
2. Bain K. What makes great teachers great? *Chron High Educ*. 2004;50(31):B7–B9.

3. Dewald NH. Transporting good library instruction practices into the web environment: An analysis of online tutorials. *J Acad Libr*. 1999;25(1):26–32.

4. Chickering AW, Gamson ZF. Seven principles for good practice in undergraduate education. *AAHE Bulletin*. 1987;39:3–7. http://www.aahea.org/aahea/articles/sevenprinciples1987.htm. Accessed February 16, 2014.

5. Dewald NH. 3.

6. Chickering AW. 4.

7. Heinich R. *Instructional Media and Technologies for Learning*. Upper Saddle River, NJ: Merrill; 2002.

8. Wiggins GP, McTighe J. *Understanding by Design*. Alexandria, VA: Association for Supervision and Curriculum Development; 1998.

9. Booth C. *Reflective Teaching, Effective Learning: Instructional Literacy for Library Educators*. Chicago, IL: American Library Association; 2011.

10. Ibid.

11. Cook D, Figurski J, Patel R, Burneo J, Langlands S, Keitz S. 6Ts teaching tips for evidence-based practitioners. *Evid Based Med*. 2007;12(4):100–101.

12. McKeachie WJ, Hofer BK, Svinicki MD. *Teaching Tips: Strategies, Research, and Theory for College and University Teachers*. Boston, MA: Houghton Mifflin; 2006.

13. Liew WM. Effects beyond effectiveness: Teaching as a performative act. *Curriculum Inquiry*. 2013;43(2):261–288.

14. Brookfield S, Preskill S. *Discussion as a Way of Teaching: Tools and Techniques for Democratic Classrooms*. San Francisco, CA: Jossey-Bass; 2005

15. Aronson L. Twelve tips for teaching reflection at all levels of medical education. *Med Teach*. 2011;33(3):200–205.

16. Ambrose SA, Bridges MW, DiPietro M, Lovett MC, Norman MK. *How Learning Works: Seven Research-Based Principles for Smart Teaching*. San Francisco, CA: Jossey-Bass; 2010.

17. Cooper JL, Robinson P. Getting started: Informal small-group strategies in large classes. *New Dir Teach & Learn*. 2000;81:17–24.

18. Crookes K, Crookes PA, Walsh K. Meaningful and engaging teaching techniques for student nurses: A literature review. *Nurse Educ Pract*. 2013;13(4):239–243.

19. Mehta NB, Hull AL, Young JB, Stoller JK. Just imagine: New paradigms for medical education. *Acad Med*. 2013;88(10):1418–1423.

12

Blended Librarianship

Daniel P. Gall

WHAT IS A BLENDED LIBRARIAN?

The call for a "blended librarian" role in academic libraries was made by Stephen Bell and John Shank in a 2004 article in *C&RL News*.[1] Their article was part of a movement toward "blended learning" that sought to combine instructional design techniques and traditional pedagogy with computer mediated instruction to promote more effective learning. Practitioners of blended learning might consider a learning goal and look at a variety of techniques and technologies before combining several of them to create a lesson. A reading assignment might be blended with an online tutorial to give background information and practical experience, for example. A class might meet in person for some lessons and online for others. Far from being a one-size-fits-all approach, blended librarianship focuses on the most effective method for delivering the desired learning outcome.

Academic librarians work in a world influenced by trends in higher education, and we often have to adapt to the preferences or goals of the instructors we work with. Rather than thinking of it as a teaching method, it is perhaps more useful to think of blended librarianship as a philosophy or way of practicing our profession. Bell and Shank's article was a response to perceived threats to librarianship caused by disruptive technologies such as Google, Amazon's book search, Questia (remember them?), and publishers bypassing the library by integrating their content directly into course management systems (CMSs). While their article did not sound a "chicken little" alarm about the end of academic librarianship, it did acknowledge that technology was changing the nature of search and the format of information. Academic librarians have traditionally excelled, they claimed, at integrating new technology while maintaining a "high touch" emphasis on user services, but we have not necessarily had as much success in our roles as educators. Shank and Bell suggested that librarians blend librarianship with the technologist's computer skills and the instructional designer's use of technology to teach effectively.[2]

While this seems a tall order, treating blended librarianship as a philosophy rather than a specific method may help. Collaboration with technologists, instructional designers, faculty, and any other useful party is encouraged in Bell and Shank's vision of blended librarianship. The blended librarian is a librarian first but is familiar enough with current technology and principles of instructional design to work effectively with partners in education. Philosophically, it is better to find the most effective means to reach your educational goal than to fit your teaching into a particular method. Blended learning, and blended librarianship, is therefore primarily practical.

BLENDED LEARNING

Blended librarianship must be understood in relation to blended learning, a pedagogy developed in the early 2000s. Blended learning, also called hybrid, is a much larger topic than we can effectively discuss in this chapter, but overviews of blended learning, including those by Allen, Seaman, and Garrett[3] and by Garrison and Vaughan,[4] are easily available online and through libraries. For purposes of this discussion, it is enough to think of blended learning as an educational movement that asked educators to evaluate their desired learning outcome for a topic or a class and then use the most effective technology and techniques to achieve that goal. It found many adherents in the growing field of distance education and became associated with blending traditional and online teaching methods.

To really understand blended learning, it helps to be familiar with pedagogy used in traditional classrooms and online. While this chapter can stand on its own, it assumes some understanding of online learning as put forth by Megan Inman and face-to-face instruction as put forth by Michele Malloy and Sarah Cantrell in other chapters of this book.

While blended librarianship can be easily defined and clearly traced to Bell and Shank, the idea of blended learning is harder to pin down to one particular educator or definition. Several influential educational organizations, including EDUCAUSE and ERIC, have developed their own definitions, and they are helpful in putting blended librarianship in context.

According to ERIC, blended learning is a

> variable construct describing approaches to teaching and learning that integrate, in a significant and meaningful way, more than one technique for delivering instruction. Widely associated with combinations of face-to-face and e-learning teaching methods, blended learning may also refer to other mixtures (e.g., individual and group instruction; self-paced instruction and lecture method).[5]

Notice that, like Bell and Shank, ERIC does not specify that blended learning must incorporate online techniques, but does point out that it is widely associated with e-learning.

EDUCAUSE specifies that blended learning include some online content, and the Sloan Consortium quantifies how much online content a course needs to meet their definition of blended.[6] One presenter at Sloan's 2013 Blended Learning Conference and Workshop held an entire session just on defining blended learning, which shows how many ways there are to interpret blended learning.[7]

All of these definitions hold in common the idea of taking the best from various teaching methods or styles, and, I argue, they are focused on the end goal of any educational enterprise, be it a specific assignment, a semester-long class, or a degree program. All the definitions emphasize the practical above anything else.

LEARNING STYLES AND BLENDED LEARNING

Howard Gardner's influential ideas about multiple intelligences have shown that people learn in different ways, and a traditional lecture is not always the most effective.[8] Recent studies using survey data[9] and analysis of CMS logs[10] have found that blended learning can positively improve learning outcomes by appealing to different learning styles.

Additionally, synchronous and asynchronous methods of communication each have their strengths and weaknesses and may be more appropriate for some learning goals than others.

Synchronous communication, such as an in-person lecture or traditional class discussion, is usually more personal; feedback is immediate, and it allows everyone in the room to easily interact with everyone else. It does not, however, easily allow people to pause when they are distracted, listen to part of the lecture again if they missed something, or save the whole thing to experience it again at their convenience. If, for example, an important meeting is scheduled during class time, you either miss class or miss the meeting.

Asynchronous communication, such as a video recording, discussion boards, or simply text on a page, lets you learn when you want to learn, pause when you like and reread or replay sections as needed. It is more difficult to be personal, however. Your teacher and classmates are still far away, and you are not with them while you learn. Feedback is not immediate. If you don't understand something, the teacher cannot see the worried expression on your face and adjust his or her teaching accordingly. You do not necessarily hear the questions and responses of your fellow students and the benefits they may provide.

A blended approach looks at the advantages and disadvantages of different technologies and communications media and tries to combine the best aspects of each.

BLENDING YOUR TEACHING

Fitting with their belief that blended librarianship was not simply a technique, but a way to think about practicing librarianship, Shank and Bell formed an online Blended Librarian Community where librarians and other educators could share ideas, ask for suggestions, and explore ways to improve their librarianship.[11] Through this site, the idea of blended librarianship has grown and morphed to meet the needs of practitioners. In many ways, the blended librarian community has become a storehouse of best practices and advice.

Given that blended learning is primarily a practical movement, the following ideas may help you conceptualize blended learning as a librarian. Keep your primary focus, of course, on the needs of your specific assignment.

- What is your goal?
    - Do specific lessons require discussion? Are there skills to be practiced with a hands-on experience or are there only facts to be digested?
    - Apply this to both the overall goals of a course and the small assignments that make up each class.
- What are your resources?
    - What technology is available to you and your students? Is there support available for you and your students if it is needed? Are there outside content experts or resources you can call on? What about your colleagues?
- What is the right technology for your need?
    - Having surveyed the available tech, what will be most effective? Is there a learning curve with it? Is it seamless for your students? Will they need particular software or equipment?
- How do you assess?
    - The need for assessment is no different in blended learning than in any other educational setting. Can you build assessment into your lesson? If you make a practical assignment, for example, will it show all the elements of learning you wish to assess?

FLIPPING THE CLASSROOM

One interesting educational trend with a similarity to blended learning is the idea of "flipping" a classroom. The idea of an inverted or flipped class has been discussed in educational literature since at least 2000,[12] but discussion increased in 2012 according to ERIC. Although still a small trend, the idea of flipping can be instructive to blended educators.

A flipped classroom is one in which the traditional "sage on the stage" classroom lecture is provided asynchronously through video, and in-person class meetings can be devoted to interaction between students and teachers, group projects, and other learning activities. Like blended learning, flipping or inverting a classroom relies on technology and is essentially practical in outlook.

It has several potential benefits:

- The teacher's time is maximized. Instead of lecturing in front of a group, the teacher can stand in front of a video camera and benefit from editing and pausing when needed.
- The student's time can be maximized. If a student does not understand part of the lecture, he can replay it at his convenience. If a student is tired or bored during class (yes, I know . . . no one is ever bored in your classes), she can take a break and listen to the lecture when she is fresh.
- Classroom time can be maximized. Instead of students sitting and listening, more emphasis is placed on doing work when the teacher is there to answer questions.

Of course, like anything, there are potential pitfalls.

- The teacher needs to find time outside class to record lectures, and editing and refining them can take time.
- The students might not actually watch the lectures.

Essentially, classroom time is flipped. The time normally devoted to homework can be done in class while the teacher is available to answer questions. The time normally devoted to lecture can be done at the convenience of the students.

PUTTING IT INTO PRACTICE

If blended learning is a practical philosophy then the best explanation of it might come from practical examples. The general concepts listed earlier are only useful when applied to real classes to give them context. The two following cases are fictionalized but based on my own experiences.

Teaching Copyright in a Blended Environment

Imagine you teach a semester-long research class at a university in the United States and want to cover copyright law. You want your students to have an understanding of the history and context of U.S. copyright law, an understanding of controversies regarding copyright, and practical knowledge they can apply to their own scholarship. Three good goals, but which methods are best for them? The strength of blended learning here is the ability to teach to the strengths of each educational goal. You do not have to choose just one method.

Your university may have many resources available to you. Perhaps there is a copyright office on campus that provides material and advice about copyright. There is a library with thousands of books and articles related to your topic, and you have colleagues who have taught this before. There is a CMS where you can host files and add links. There is a teaching support center where you can find an instructional designer who might help you think through and refine your lesson. The instructional technology services department provides computer support and networking. There are also many websites and public domain sources of information about copyright.

There is some useful information available through the Copyright Office, but it seems to be geared more toward protecting the intellectual property of faculty and researchers. You talk with your colleagues and learn that one of them just found a book chapter discussing copyright case law that provides an excellent overview of U.S. copyright law including the TEACH Act, Digital Millennium Copyright Act (DMCA), and other important pieces of legislation. You also remember a conference presentation that showed a short video with a Creative Commons license that briefly explains how copyright law developed before it explains Creative Commons.

You're starting to get some ideas now about how to teach this lesson, but you're not sure what to do about making copyright information practical for your students. You make an appointment with a friendly instructional designer who shows you an interactive game feature in the CMS and, suddenly, all the pieces of your lesson start coming together.

You assign the Creative Commons video and book chapter to your students as a pre-class assignment. In class, you ask them about the video and readings and then divide the class into small groups representing content producers (artists, scholars, etc.), content distributors (publishing and film companies), and consumers. They need to find an acceptable consensus about who owns the content, for how long, and so on. You evaluate their discussion. Finally, as a homework assignment your students will play the Copyright Lawyer game you developed with the instructional designer.

Blending for Convenience

Let us suppose you teach the same semester-long course at the same university in the United States, but this time let us say your class meets one night a week for three hours at an off-campus location several hours away. Most of your students are working adults who come to class after their full eight-hour work day and about half of them travel for more than an hour to reach the classroom. What is the most effective way to reach these students? How can you minimize your own commute to the remote location and still teach effectively?

Your goals in this case might be much broader when looking at the whole semester, but you evaluate your syllabus to see what you want to accomplish each week. You notice some weeks where the topics you want to cover lend themselves to individual effort and some weeks where the topics are more suited to group activity. You believe everyone in your class has something to teach the others, even if they don't yet know what, and want to encourage your students to communicate with each other and form a learning community.

As in our first scenario, your resources include instructional designers and IT support, a CMS, and your colleagues. You also have the classroom, which has chairs that can be moved into various configurations.

In general, your technology resources can be divided into classroom technology and networked technology, which is mostly available through the CMS. It includes e-mail, chat, discussion boards, file storage, a calendar, links to campus resources, and many other potentially useful things.

You decide to structure the class so that you only meet in person every three weeks. Before class begins you contact your students by e-mail to explain the class schedule and set expectations. They are assigned to familiarize themselves with the discussion board by introducing themselves there and asking questions of at least two other students. In the first class meeting, you ask everyone to pick up their desk chairs and arrange themselves into a circle rather than rows. The time the class spends together in person must focus on working as groups and interaction—it is important that they feel comfortable with each other and that they can make the classroom their home for the duration of the class session.

You arrange your semester such that for two weeks assignments and readings are done individually and discussion happens through the discussion board. On the third week, you and your students travel to the off-campus classroom in person. Although there is a learning curve for interacting successfully on the discussion board, your students say they appreciate your respect for their time and schedules. They seem to see the class meetings as a finite resource and want to make the most of it when they are there.

Blended learning is not very explicit in these hypothetical examples. No one sat down with the goal of "blending" something. Instead, the blending happened as the teacher looked for the most practical and effective ways to teach specific material. When done best, it is an organic process but it requires planning and care—just like any class.

RESOURCES FOR BLENDED LEARNING

Sticking with our practical theme, perhaps the best place to look for blended learning resources is within your own institution. The term *blended learning* might not be that helpful at your institution if no one else uses it, but many institutions have blended learning resources in place without calling them that. Talk to teaching support personnel in the instructional technology department to see what technology is available to you. Find out what your institution does for teacher development and if there are instructional designers available at your institution. Find out from your colleagues what effective teaching strategies they use. Be creative.

Bell and Shank's online Blended Librarian Community has grown since its beginnings in 2004 and is available at http://blendedlibrarian. learningtimes.net. Blended librarians have used the discussion boards to ask advice, propose ideas, solve problems, and support one another. The record of their discussions can be very useful. For a practical outline of blended learning not limited to the library, try the Blended Learning

Toolkit at http://blended.online.ucf.edu. Additionally, both the Sloan Consortium (http://sloanconsortium.org) and EDUCAUSE (http://www.educause.edu/) hold conferences or workshops on blended learning and have publications and research on the topic.

CONCLUSION

Are you a blended librarian? If you are more interested in whether you accomplish your educational goal than whether you call yourself blended, then you may already be a blended librarian. If your focus is on the most effective way to teach, then you may already be a blended librarian. If you are a problem solver and want to use technology to make your teaching more accessible and efficient for your students, you may already be a blended librarian. Welcome to the community.

NOTES

1. Bell SJ, Shank J. The blended librarian: A blueprint for redefining the teaching and learning role of academic librarians. *C & RL News*. 2004; 65:372–375.

2. Ibid.

3. Allen IE, Seaman J, Garrett R. Blending in: The extent and promise of blended education in the United States. Sloan Consortium website. http://sloanconsortium.org/publications/survey/blended06. Published March, 2007. Accessed December 9, 2013.

4. Garrison DR, Vaughan, ND. *Blended Learning in Higher Education: Framework, Principles, and Guidelines*. San Francisco, CA: Jossey-Bass; 2008.

5. ERIC. Blended learning. ERIC Thesaurus. http://eric.ed.gov/?qt=blended +learning&ti=Blended+Learning. Published July 8, 2008. Accessed December 13, 2013.

6. EDUCAUSE. Blended learning. http://www.educause.edu/library/blended-learning. Accessed December 13, 2013.

7. Guarcello M. Reconsidering definition "blended." Sloan Consortium website. http://sloanconsortium.org/conference/2013/blended/reconsidering-definition-blended. Published July 2013. Accessed December 13, 2013.

8. Gardner H. The theory of multiple intelligences. *Annals of Dyslexia*. 1987, 37:19–35.

9. Lopez S, Patron H. Multiple intelligences in online, hybrid, and traditional business statistics courses. *J Educ Online*. 2012, 9(2):1–16.

10. Mogus AM, Djurdjevic I, Suvak N. The impact of student activity in a virtual learning environment on their final mark. *Active Learn Higher Educ*. 2012, 13(3):177–189.

11. Blended Librarian website. http://blendedlibrarian.learningtimes.net/about-bl/. Accessed December 18, 2013.

12. Lage MJ, Platt GJ, Treglia M. Inverting the classroom: A gateway to creating an inclusive learning environment. *J Econ Educ*. 2000, 31(1):30–43.

13

Incorporating Self-Assessment and Peer Assessment into Library Instructional Practice

Stephan J. Macaluso

Assessment is an important element in curricular design. Library educators use a wide variety of techniques to assess whether students have met their instructional objectives. The feedback they receive via student work products and student attitudinal surveys provide insights into whether the learning experience has contributed to students' abilities to apply information literacy strategies or develop their confidence in independent research. These measures can in turn assist the library educator in the development of new learning outcomes, and the improvement of one's instructional materials and classroom technique. Some libraries have had great success in using assessment data to inform whether a curricular change was warranted.[1,2]

While these measures can demonstrate whether the library instruction program is meeting its goals, no single assessment tool or strategy provides a comprehensive look at student learning outcomes, application of new skills, or areas where the instructor him- or herself may improve. Some studies suggest that students retain little of the information taught in library instruction programs; work products also present an incomplete picture of the library's educational impact.[3(p265)] Moreover, libraries often employ tools that measure user satisfaction or self-confidence in library skills rather than the application of those skills.

A more balanced and comprehensive curricular evaluation emerges when student learning outcomes and attitudinal measurements are partnered with library educator self-reflection and peer assessment. Some libraries have embraced such multifaceted approaches,[4] while some studies indicate that a mixed-methodology approach paints a richer picture of student learning.[5,6]

This chapter will demonstrate some techniques that a library educator may employ to reflect upon his or her instructional methods, tools, and strategies. It will then explore some of the methods commonly employed in peer evaluation of one's instruction. When used in combination with student learning measures, these techniques may play a strong role in programmatic assessment and development.

SELF-EVALUATION/SELF REFLECTION

Library educators may associate self-assessment with annual reporting or dossier review. Such assessments draw from a variety of sources: for example, student outcomes data and work products; student evaluations of instruction; or informal conversations with peers and supervisors. One may also reflect on one's professional activities—for example, one's classroom teaching methods and materials.

The greater purpose of self-reflection is to develop a sense of where one's strengths and areas for improvement lie and what steps one might take to improve or grow as an educator. Honest self-reflection on what one believes one has accomplished, or on how one's instructional policies, practices, strategies, and techniques affect student learning are an important driver in instructional improvement.[7(p193–196)] Some institutions sponsor faculty retreats to facilitate self-reflection.

While some models for librarian self-reflective practice have been proposed[8] and others may be adapted from the education literature,[9,10,11] there are relatively few field reports about how librarians become reflective teachers, or what methods they employ to self-assess their work. Doherty[12] draws upon Paulo Freire, Henry Giroux, and others, to propose a framework by which librarians periodically examine their personal and professional assumptions through intentional student-instructor dialogue.

Through self-reflection and professional reading, McDonald[13] examined how the metaphors she had long used to describe her professional role (e.g., drill sergeant and accidental educator) were out of sync with her own teaching and learning preferences. These metaphors had been reinforced by the pace and limits of her one-shot library classes. She came to recognize that, as a result, she had at times been too prescriptive in her teaching and realized she needed to evolve a greater variety of teaching methods that were more akin to her own personal style of learning. This resulted in a positive change in her relationship with her students and her curriculum.

Whether one uses a philosophical framework or a personal metaphor as a touchstone, self-reflection can play an important role in the development of one's teaching. A variety of short writing exercises and list-making tools can facilitate one's self-reflection. These exercises promote metacognition. Metacognition may be defined as the ability to better understand how one learns and, by extension, prepares for and reacts to what one teaches. These exercises also promote synthesis, which may be defined as the ability to incorporate what one has learned into one's professional life.[14]

Brookfield[15] offers a number of exercises with which library educators can record their observations and respond to reflective prompts regarding their teaching. These exercises have much in common with "minute papers" that are often assigned to students to prompt their own reflection. While they play an important role in our professional development when administered to our classes, they act as a unique self-reflective inventory when librarians complete them.

Brookfield's Critical Incident Questionnaire (CIQ)[16(p115)] has been used most famously with students in library settings by Gilstrap and Dupree.[17(p114)] The purpose of the CIQ is not to determine what students liked or disliked about the class but rather what they found most significant. When CIQs are collected and reviewed by the instructor, they offer valuable insights into one's teaching—for example, whether there are gaps between what one intended to teach and what the students found most meaningful. Moreover, additional insights are gained when the instructor completes a CIQ him- or herself and compares those findings with those of the class as a whole.

The CIQ is a five-question inventory; I propose that an equal benefit may be obtained by altering the questions slightly, to include the following:

- What was the moment I felt most in touch with this class?
- What prompted me to think at some point that the students really "got it"?

- What was the one point when I felt it was very difficult to get a concept or skill across to the students?
- What do I recall about what I said? What verbal and nonverbal feedback do I recall receiving?

Brookfield suggests that instructors use teaching logs to periodically respond to questions such as "What would I do differently next time I teach this class?"; "What surprised me most about this class?"; and "What gave me the most trouble?"[18(p72)] "Learning audits" ask instructors to reflect on their teaching over time.[19(p75–77)] Most creatively, "survival memos" ask the instructor to write a note to one's successor, outlining how specific resources, instructor knowledge, and methods contributed to the success of a class (i.e., which the successor should try) and the missteps one should avoid.[20(p79)] While autobiographical and deeply personal, these reflections may be shared in some form with colleagues in a teaching circle or with a mentor to test common assumptions, develop a common set professional development needs, or review concerns about teaching and curriculum.[21(p74)]

Visually oriented library educators may find cause-effect diagrams, plus/delta exercises, and force-field diagrams to be valuable self-assessment tools. While traditionally used in group settings,[22] they may be adapted for use by individual instructors. These simple variations on list-making tools work well for recording basic information about a library session and create opportunities for reflection. By recording the information and saving this with course materials, one can reflect on patterns in one's teaching that emerge over time.

Cause-effect diagrams are often employed to help discern the root causes of a problem.[23(p25–27)] Known also as fishbone diagrams because they resemble a fish skeleton, each "spine" represents a dimension of a situation or experience: for example, technology, environment, or materials. With slight variation, cause-effect diagrams can provide an efficient record of one's observations that can be used for personal reflection or may be shared with a colleague or mentor.

Plus/delta[24(p97–102)] exercises are a variation on making a list of pros and cons, but instead of listing the negatives of a situation, one lists what one desires to change in order to improve an experience. I have used plus/delta in library workshops to evaluate specific research tools (e.g., what are the pros of X database or resource? What would you need to change about your research process to make X database work more effectively?) Ideally, the instructor should plus/delta the library session with the class. By design, this tool captures a lot of diverse information quickly including student reactions to the session or environmental and technological factors impacting the session. The plus/delta can be used as a self-assessment tool, or can be completed with a mentor, peer observer, or collaborating instructor.

A force-field diagram[25(p59)] is typically used to discover the drivers and barriers to an initiative. In a library instruction setting one may describe what appeared to propel the class forward (e.g., a provocative question, a well-prepared group of students, or a flashy presentation). One can then describe what appeared to slow the lesson's momentum (e.g., a technical malfunction, a poorly chosen demonstration topic, or students' late arrival to class.) Using force-field diagramming individually requires the instructor to be keenly aware of the conditions of the space in which one is working, the timing of one's presentation, and nonverbal and verbal feedback that one gets from the class.

Suskie[26(p173)] offers a two-part self-reflection technique that has much in common with peer observation techniques (of which, more later). Before the teaching session the instructor makes a list that may include the class's attributes (e.g., class size, level and sample topics if known, time of day); instructional objectives and a summary of one's preparations; the tools, techniques, and technologies he or she intends to use; and how learning is to be assessed. After the class, the instructor records in as detailed a manner as possible what took place, including the challenges he or she faced and how he or she responded; lingering questions the instructor has about what was learned or what was left out of the session and why; and how the instructor's expectations for the class aligned with what really happened. From this comparison, the library educator should discover one or more things to do differently in the future.

PEER EVALUATION AND FACULTY FEEDBACK

Peer Observation

While peer observation has been used by some academic libraries for personnel review,[27,28] it is more commonly used as a formative assessment strategy intended to improve instructional technique.

Many institutions employ a three-part observation method. Part 1 often involves a pre-observation conversation, in which paired colleagues discuss the prospective teaching strategies and outcomes of an upcoming class. Part 2 is the observation itself. Part 3 is often a post-observation conference where the pair discusses what was observed. Depending upon how formal (and how confidential) the process, subsequent steps might include additional observations or targeted professional development.

Weimer cautions that in college settings, observation has too often been a summative process, performed by administrators or department chairs.[29(p120,121)] Observation results may be influenced by the prior experience of the observer, and there may be lingering apprehensions about how the results are to be used. While increasingly used for collegial improvement of one's teaching, it is not unusual to find that colleagues are unwilling to participate in peer observation. Training through a campus center for teaching excellence, or a low-stakes pilot among like-minded colleagues can alleviate those concerns. Libraries may also consider these strategies in order to encourage participation:

1. Develop clear policies regarding the format of observation reports: who receives them, what their intent is, and what they may or may not be used for.
2. Provide observers with checklists or rubrics; identify specific areas on which to provide feedback.
3. Encourage new faculty to observe experienced effective instructors. Observation can demonstrate how an experienced instructor confronts the variety of classroom challenges.
4. Volunteer to be observed by an expert: while not strictly a "peer" review, campus teaching excellence centers or instructional designers may be available to observe teaching sessions.
5. Encourage a review of one's class materials, for example, websites or other learning objects, in lieu of one's classroom teaching. The Association for College and Research Libraries' PRIMO program is one of many outlets for the review of instructional content.

At SUNY New Paltz, librarians first piloted a three-part peer observation initiative during the 2002 academic year. Librarians are paired with peers who agree to observe each other's classes two or more times during a semester. The results are confidential and designed solely for professional development: no information about the observations is placed in a personnel file.

Pre-observation discussion is often driven by the following prompts:

- Three objectives for my class are . . .
- Three things I would like your feedback on are . . .
- One thing I would not like feedback on is . . .
- My overall impression about how successful I will be is . . . because . . .

The library developed an optional form to facilitate the observation. It captures how the instructor used teaching materials and technology, and how the instructor promoted classroom discussion. An instructor self-assessment form was devised to facilitate post-conference discussion. Its prompts include the following:

- Some of the ways I prepared for this class were . . .
- I "got a reading" of the class's experiences and skills by . . .
- The main points I wanted to get across to the class were . . .
- The things I feel I did especially well include . . .
- One insight I gained from this session was . . .
- Two things I would like to improve for next time are . . .

Libraries have applied other successful observation models. Ozek and associates employed a "critical friend" strategy. Their volunteer-driven initiative leveraged a high degree of staff trust and began with substantial training in peer observation, collegial conversation, and teaching methods conducted by the campus center for teaching and learning.[30] A critical friend was "a trusted person who asks provocative questions . . . and offers a critique of the person's work as a friend."[31(p19)] The observation pairs spent significant time together, discussing best practices for teaching library concepts. The initiative resulted in several insights and areas for personal improvement among the instructor-participants. These included greater confidence and a decreased sense of isolation; an affirmation of their instructional practices; and a greater sensitivity to their interactions with students.

The University of Colorado at Boulder employed a peer-coaching model in which the peer observer was trained to facilitate the observed-teacher's self-reflection.[32] A multifaceted training program was designed to affirm common pedagogical values, build reflective practice, and address confidentiality issues among the participants. Observations were driven by the teacher-observers' stated needs; coaches used logs, time maps, predefined behavior checklists, and five-minute interval checks of students' behaviors to record the observations. One of the reported results was a greater sense of reflectiveness among those being observed. This initiative helped the library to better articulate its curricular goals.

Finley and associates describe the program at the University of Nevada, Las Vegas, in which coaching, teaching circles, and team-teaching combine into a more holistic peer-reviewed experience.[33] Instructors who desired to incorporate new strategies into their library classes brainstormed with an in-house educational enhancement team and were later paired with team members for in-class assistance and feedback. Participants reported that the program helped develop a sense of self-reflection and of shared curricular goals. Other reported results included a greater willingness to experiment with teaching techniques and a willingness to share those new techniques with colleagues at brown-bag events.

Although video technology (e.g., screencasts, live lecture capture, or simulations) has become commonplace in library instruction, the literature on its use in self- and peer evaluation is surprisingly thin. Brooks Doherty and Anne Deutsch ("Caught in the Act: Video Classroom Observation," Presentation, ACRL 2013) led a cadre of library educators who had their library sessions recorded and uploaded to a secure learning management system, and participated in a round-robin critique of one another's teaching. This was a decidedly low-stakes, formative assessment, but even under those conditions, it may be challenging to find instructors who are willing to submit to such a review. Reluctant instructors may alternatively get their feet wet by watching and critiquing one of the many instructional videos available online (e.g., YouTube). Watching with a mentor or peer may encourage prospective observees to be video recorded/observed and help to negotiate on which aspects of their session they desire feedback most from their observer. Moreover, the prospective observer can use the premade video to field test his or her observational technique.

In sum, formative and collegial peer observation can provide guidance to library instructors regarding teaching technique and promote library-wide reflection on curriculum and, ultimately, student success.

Feedback by Disciplinary Faculty

Walter has made the observation that professorial faculty often share the same concerns about classroom management, time management, content delivery, and assessment as library instructors.[34] Library instruction sessions can provide a rich opportunity for collegial feedback from the course instructor on one's teaching. Many faculty members may be quite willing to offer feedback, especially those with whom the librarian has some prior familiarity or has a department that practices peer observation.

Libraries have frequently deployed online questionnaire-style forms to gather faculty feedback. These forms offer several benefits. They can be completed quickly. They can be customized for specific disciplines, levels, and library experiences. Merely creating a feedback form allows the library to clarify its values, as the questions that are asked speak to what it values the most, whether hands-on time with the database or time spent with the library special collection or personal connections made between the library instructor and the students; what constitutes efficient use of instructional time and what the library values will be priorities for the survey. Faculty feedback forms may also (inferentially) remind the professor to reinforce library instruction concepts, solicit student feedback, or invite students to take advantage of other library services.

Despite these affordances, library educators may prefer the more open-ended, dialogical feedback that comes from direct observation and debriefing by a disciplinary colleague. Professors who are amenable but time constrained may be asked to observe specific attributes of the class and address more intentional, domain-specific questions. Targeted questions on specific dimensions of the class meeting can help bypass questions like "Did you like it?" and "Did I cover enough?" in favor of ones that prompt self-reflection on whether the students learned what one intended to teach, and that enable dialogue with the discipline (e.g., is this how students tend to learn this material?).[35(p153)] Some targeted prompts that the professor might address include the following:

- What did you think of my using X to demonstrate that concept?
- What do you think the students appreciated most?
- Was there a point when you thought I may have confused some of the students?
- What features of this session were useful for you, personally?
- What do you think will require the most reinforcement or follow-up? How would we best accomplish that?
- How might you reinforce what we learned about the importance of (reference books, citation) in your classroom?

One might also consider asking disciplinary and curricular-minded questions, which may include the following:

- What aspects of research (e.g., issues with access, synthesizing data) do you talk about in your classes or in your discipline? What are the emerging issues?
- How did my metaphors, analogies, and search techniques accord with the ones you would have used if you were leading this session?
- If we could add one thing to this session, what would it be?
- If we could take away one thing, what would it be?
- If we could move one facet of this session online, what might it be?

Finally, enlisting the help of departmental faculty can demonstrate your desire to play a greater role in curricular assessment. Ongoing campus dialogue may create opportunities for the library to collaborate with departments on additional assessment activities and curricular improvement.

CONCLUSION

When used in harmony with student assessments, the self-reflection and colleague observation strategies described in this chapter create a rich and insightful picture of how a library educator's techniques and materials meet their pedagogical goals. Through self-reflective critical assessment, the instructor challenges his or her assumptions. Collegial peer observation and feedback from institutional colleagues promote professional growth while helping to develop reflection and intentional conversation about the library's instructional curriculum.

NOTES

1. Gilstrap DL, Dupree J. Assessing learning, critical reflection, and quality educational outcomes: The Critical Incident Questionnaire. *Coll & Res Libr.* 2008;69(5):407–426.

2. Swoger BJM. Closing the assessment loop using pre- and post-assessment. *Ref Serv Rev.* 2011;39(2):244–259.

3. Schilling K, Applegate R. Best methods for evaluating educational impact: A comparison of the efficacy of commonly used measures of library instruction. *J Med Libr Assoc.* 2012;100(4):258–269.

4. Snavely L, DeWald N. Perspective on . . . developing and implementing peer review of academic librarians' teaching: An overview and case report. *J Acad Libr.* 2011;37(4):343–351.

5. Bowles-Terry M. Library instruction and academic success: A mixed-methods assessment of a library instruction program. *Evid Based Libr & Inf Pract.* 2012;7(1):82–95.

6. Julien H, Boon S. Assessing instructional outcomes in Canadian academic libraries. *Libr & Inf Sci Res.* 2004;26(2):121–39.

7. Weimer M. *Learner-Centered Teaching: Five Key Changes to Practice.* San Francisco, CA: Jossey-Bass, 2002.

8. Booth C. *Reflective Teaching, Effective Learning: Instructional Literacy for Library Educators.* Chicago, IL: American Library Association; 2011.

9. Marzano RJ. *Classroom Assessment and Grading That Work.* Alexandria, VA: Association for Supervision and Curriculum Development; 2006.

10. Brookfield SD. *Becoming a Critically Reflective Teacher.* San Francisco, CA: Jossey-Bass; 1995.

11. Handal G, Lauvås P. *Promoting Reflective Teaching: Supervision in Practice.* Philadelphia, PA: Open University Press; 1987.

12. Doherty JJ. Towards self-reflection in librarianship: What is praxis? *Progressive Libr.* 2005/2006;26:11–17.

13. Macdonald K. Out of the boot camp and into the chrysalis: A reflective practice case study. *Aust Libr J.* 2009: 17–27.

14. Suskie L. *Assessing Student Learning: A Common Sense Guide.* San Francisco, CA: Anker; 2004.

15. Brookfield SD. 10.

16. Ibid.

17. Gilstrap DL. 1.

18. Brookfield SD. 10.

19. Ibid.

20. Ibid.

21. Ibid.

22. Laughlin S, Shockley DS, Wilson R. *The Library's Continuous Improvement Fieldbook: Twenty-Nine Ready-to-Use Tools*. Chicago, IL: American Library Association; 2003.

23. Ibid.

24. Ibid.

25. bid.

26. Suskie L. 14.

27. Middleton C. Evolution of peer evaluation of library instruction at Oregon State University libraries. *portal: Libr & Academy*. 2002; 2(1):69–78.

28. Fielden N, Foster M. Crossing the rubricon: Evaluating the information literacy instructor. *J Inform Literacy*. 2010;42(2):78–90.

29. Weimer, M. *Improving Your Classroom Teaching*. Newbury Park, CA: Sage, 1993.

30. Ozek, YH, Edgren G, Jander K. Implementing the critical friend method for peer feedback among teaching librarians in an academic setting. *Evid Based Libr & Inf Pract*. 2012:7(4):68–81.

31. Ibid.

32. Sinkinson C. An assessment of peer coaching to drive professional development and reflective teaching. *Commun Inform Literacy*. 2011;5(1):9–20.

33. Finley P, Skarl S, Cox J, VanderPol D. Enhancing library instruction with peer planning. *Ref Serv Rev*. 2005;33(1):112–122.

34. Walter S. Instructional improvement: building capacity for the professional development of librarians as teachers. *Ref & User Serv Q*. 2006;45(3): 213–218.

35. Suskie L. 14.

ADDITIONAL RECOMMENDED READING

Brookfield SD, Preskill S. *Discussion as a Way of Teaching: Tools and Techniques for Democratic Classrooms*. San Francisco, CA: Jossey-Bass; 1999.

Bryan JE, Karshmer E. Assessment in the one-shot session: Using pre- and post-tests to measure innovative instructional strategies among first-year students. *Coll & Res Libr*.2013;74(6):574–586.

Cross KP, Angelo TA. *Classroom Assessment Techniques: A Handbook for College Teachers*. San Francisco, CA: Jossey-Bass; 1993.

Diamond RM. *Designing and Assessing Courses and Curricula: A Practical Guide*. San Francisco, CA: Jossey-Bass; 1998.

Hart D. *Authentic Assessment: A Handbook for Educators*. Menlo Park, CA: Addison Wesley; 1994.

Hsieh ML, Dawson PH, Carlin MT. What five minutes in the classroom can do to uncover the basic information literacy skills of your college students: A multiyear assessment study. *Evid Based Libr & Inf Pract*. 2013;8(3):34–57.

Lindauer BG. The three arenas of information literacy. *Ref & User Serv Q*. 2004;44(2):122–129.

McKeachie WJ, Svinicki M. *McKeachie's Teaching Tips: Strategies, Research, and Theory for College and University Teachers*. 12th ed. Boston, MA: Houghton Mifflin; 2006.

Marzano RJ, Boogren T, Heflebower T, Kanold-McIntyre J, Pickering D. *Becoming a Reflective Teacher*. Bloomington, IN: Marzano Research Laboratory; 2012.

Oakleaf M. Dangers and opportunities: A conceptual map of information literacy assessment approaches. *portal: Libr & Academy*. 2008;8(3):233–253.

Smale MA, Regalado M. Using Blackboard to deliver library research skills assessment. *Communications in Information Literacy*. 2009;3(2):142–157.

V

**SUBJECT-BASED INSTRUCTION
IN HEALTH SCIENCES**

14

Evidence-Based Medicine and Medical Students

Connie Schardt

Picture this: One of your medical students is volunteering at an inner-city well child clinic. It is Saturday afternoon and she is examining an 18-month-old child with an inflamed ear who is obviously in some discomfort. The mother is concerned about the earache but also about giving her child unnecessary medications. The medical student thinks this is otitis media and confirms the diagnosis with the medical director. The medical director asks the student what she plans to do for the child. The student is uncertain as to whether an antibiotic, such as Amoxicillin, is appropriate for this case. She remembers a lecture on overprescribing antibiotics and otitis media as an example of this problem in a pediatric population. But the student is not sure whether this very young patient, under the age of two years, might nonetheless benefit from drug therapy. She needs to quickly find additional accurate information that will help her and the mother of the child decide on the best course of care. The medical student needs to be able to conceptualize the medical dilemma into a clinical question, to efficiently search for reliable information, and to evaluate that information for its validity and applicability to the specific patient problem. Is your medical student prepared to do this?

WHAT IS EVIDENCE-BASED PRACTICE?

It all started in the early 1990s with evidence-based medicine (EBM), which was defined as a way of practicing medicine that explicitly

incorporates current and valid medical research along with patient preferences and values into the process of making sound clinical decisions
and as a way of making sure that clinicians have an effective strategy
for lifelong learning that improves patient care[1,2] This "new" paradigm
for making health care decisions and managing current information was
soon adopted by other health care practitioners, including nurses, physical therapists, dentists, and physician assistants. This broader approach,
evidence-based practice (EBP), allows all practitioners of health care "to
critically assess research data, clinical guidelines, and other information
resources in order to correctly identify the clinical problem, apply the
most high-quality intervention, and re-evaluate the outcome for future
improvement."[3] See figure 14.1 for a diagram summarizing the process.

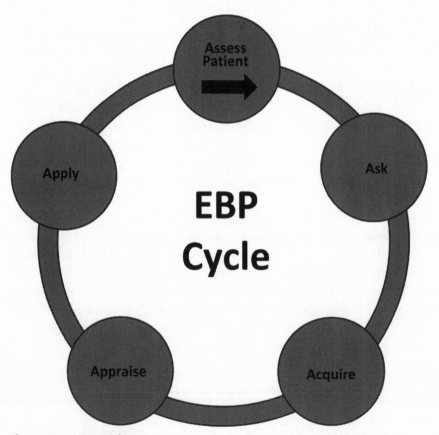

Figure 14.1. EBP Cycle

EBP begins and ends with a patient and has a formalized process to follow. Step 1 is to *assess* the patient situation and acknowledge possible uncertainty. This includes the physical examination, a discussion with the patient or caregiver, and an understanding of the urgency and magnitude of the problem. When there is uncertainty as to how to proceed or which intervention might be the most beneficial to the patient, EBP can provide a road map to help resolve the dilemma.

Step 2 is to *ask* a focused and answerable clinical question. Depending on the learner there may be several clinical questions that arise out of a patient encounter. Some of these questions, especially for new learners, will be background questions and require textbook or summary information. Background questions usually have two components—a query such as "what is" or "how does" and a condition, syndrome, or pathophysiology. On the other hand, foreground questions ask for specific information to inform clinical decisions about a specific patient or particular population. Foreground questions tend to be more complex compared to background questions and ask for more information:

P—the specific patient problem, condition or disease
I—the intervention, which can be a drug therapy, a surgical procedure, a diagnostic test or other prognostic factor
C—the comparison, if deciding between two different interventions
O—the outcome or desired result, which will benefit the patient[4]

This is referred to as PICO and helps the learner remember the important parts of a well-built clinical question.[5]

Step 3 is to *acquire* the information that will address the clinical question. This dictates that the learner has access to high-quality, accurate, and current medical information. This also means that the learner has the necessary skills to translate the PICO into a search strategy and to quickly find specific information. There are numerous resources to help with this step, such as DynaMed, Clinical Evidence, UpToDate, and ACP Journal Club, which make it easier for the learner by evaluating and summarizing current information on common topics. Other resources such as PubMed or CINAHL (Cumulative Index to Nursing and Allied Health Literature) are more comprehensive and provide access to the primary biomedical literature.

Step 4 is to *appraise* the information that is acquired. While there are secondary resources that do evaluate the quality of the information presented, they do not answer every possible clinical question. Very often the learner will need to go to the primary literature to identify information that addresses the clinical question.[6] Appraising the validity of a primary study means understanding the important criteria for each specific type of study and determining whether it was done properly to eliminate potential biases that could compromise the results.

Step 5 is to *apply* the results of critically appraised information to the clinical decision by incorporating the evidence and the patient's preferences and values into the discussion. "The practice of evidence based medicine is a process of life-long, self-directed learning in which caring for our patients creates the need for clinically important information about diagnosis, prognosis therapy and other health related issues."[7(p2–3)] EBP may require new skills and a change in behavior and attitude that can be best facilitated by a variety of educational interventions throughout medical school.

WHAT RESPONSIBILITY DO MEDICAL SCHOOLS HAVE FOR MAKING SURE THEIR STUDENTS CAN PRACTICE EBP?

Entities that provide guidance and accreditation to medical schools have recognized EBP as an important skill and responsibility for physicians. The American Association of Medical Colleges provides guidance to medical schools through its Medical School Objectives Project. The current guidelines for medical schools clearly state, "Physicians must apply the principles of evidence-based medicine and cost effectiveness in making decisions about the utilization of limited medical resources."[8] To that end the medical school "must ensure that before graduation a student will have demonstrated, to the satisfaction of the faculty . . . the ability to retrieve (from electronic databases and other resources), manage, and utilize biomedical information for solving problems and making decisions that are relevant to the care of individuals and population."[9]

The Liaison Committee on Medical Education (LCME) is recognized by the U.S. Department of Education as the reliable authority for the accreditation of medical education programs leading to the MD degree. The

LCME recently completed a reorganization of its accreditation standards. Standard 7 focuses on curricular content and includes two standards that relate to EBP:

7.3 [ED-12/ED-17-A]. CURRICULAR CONTENT: SCIENTIFIC METHOD/CLINICAL/TRANSLATIONAL RESEARCH. The faculty of an institution that sponsors a medical education program ensures that the program's curriculum includes instruction in the scientific method (including hands-on or simulated exercises in which medical students collect or use data to test and/or verify hypotheses or address questions about biomedical phenomena) and in the basic scientific and ethical principles of clinical and translational research (including the ways in which such research is conducted, evaluated, explained to patients, and applied to patient care).

7.4 [ED-6]. CURRICULAR CONTENT: CRITICAL JUDGMENT/PROBLEM-SOLVING SKILLS. The faculty of an institution that sponsors a medical education program ensures that the program's curriculum incorporates the fundamental principles of medicine, provides opportunities for medical students to acquire skills of critical judgment based on evidence and experience, and develops medical students' ability to use principles and skills effectively in solving problems of health and disease.[10]

Both of these agencies have placed a high value on educating medical students to be lifelong learners through effective utilization of the biomedical literature.

WHAT IS THE MOST EFFECTIVE WAY
TO TEACH THESE SKILLS AND CHANGE BEHAVIOR?

Many different strategies have been used for teaching evidence-based medicine, including didactic lectures, journal clubs, stand-alone self-paced tutorials, and reading textbooks.[11,12,13,14] However studies have shown that these strategies are not very effective and do not result in changed behavior. Coomarasamy and Khan addressed this issue in a systematic review that examined the effects of stand-alone versus clinically integrated teaching on various outcomes (knowledge, critical appraisal skills, attitudes, and behavior) in postgraduates.[15] After a thorough review of the literature they identified 23 studies that "evaluated the effects of postgraduate EBM or critical appraisal teaching compared with a control group or baseline before teaching, using a measure of participants' learning achievements or patients' health gains as outcomes." While the quality of the studies varied, their findings showed that both stand-alone courses and integrated teaching improved knowledge but improvements in skills, attitudes, and behavior came about when teaching was integrated into clinical practice. Many medical schools have adopted the integrated approach to teaching EBM that creates a longitudinal learning experience that is threaded throughout coursework and clinical rotations.[16,17,18,19,20]

With further research, Khan and Coomarasamy developed a hierarchical approach to teaching and learning EBM based on current empirical and theoretical evidence.[21] They proposed three levels of teaching and learning: the top level is interactive and integrated teaching and learning activities; the middle level is either interactive classroom-based teaching or didactic, but clinically integrated learning activities; and the bottom level is classroom or stand-alone teaching. In addition, they identified criteria related to medical education that would enhance its value for the learner:

- Learning incorporated into clinical practice
- Sequenced events that aid reinforcement, rather than single or episodic events
- Education that identifies and takes into account learner needs
- Multifaceted strategies in teaching and learning
- Education that gives individual feedback and the opportunity for self-assessment

WHY IS THIS IMPORTANT FOR LIBRARIANS?

The practitioner of EBP must have specific skills and resources to be successful in managing medical information. Medical school standards and guidelines dictate that students be taught these skills, which focus on acquiring and applying medical information in the care of patients. Managing information requires that the information need is recognized and understood, that the best sources for answering the question are identified and available, and that the quality of the information is evaluated before applying it back to the patient problem. These research skills closely parallel the information management components that are part of the professional competencies of health sciences librarians.[22]

The practice of EBP impacts library services through collection development, which provides access to relevant resources (textbooks, point-of-care, and databases) and education services, which teaches medical students the skills to formulate focused questions, to identify the best resources, to formulate effective search strategies, and to evaluate the quality of the information. Slawson and Shaughnessy have argued that "there is a need to teach the applied science of information management along with, or perhaps even instead of, teaching the basic science of EBM."[23]

The process of EBP should be introduced to medical students in incremental steps based on the immediate educational needs of the students. Medical students during their first year of study may not be managing patient care but still need the information management and research skills embedded in EBP to complete course assignments. This is the time to start teaching students about the value of the resources and effective searching skills for the more complex databases. Once the students begin to see patients during their clinical rotations, this instruction can be framed around specific patient cases to answer real clinical questions and introduce the concept of EBP. The next logical step is to teach critical appraisal skills so that students can evaluate the literature and make relevant contributions to their patient care teams. This longitudinal or integrated approach allows for learning based on the immediate educational objective and allows for exploring a variety of teaching modalities, including interactive small groups, case-based online modules, journal clubs, and team-based learning. It also reinforces the concepts by repetition in a variety of settings from the classroom to the bedside where it has the greatest potential to affect patient care. Many academic medical libraries are involved in teaching all or some of the EBP skills to students, often in partnership with clinicians.[24,25,26,27,28] Table 14.1 shows an example of a longitudinal approach to teaching EBP principles to medical students based on a proposal from the Medical Center Library (Duke University). The sessions are integrated into existing classroom instruction and clinical rotations throughout the four years. Depending on the session, facilitators and instructors are librarians and/or clinical faculty.

Table 14.1. Sample Integrated EBM Course

Integrated Approach to Teaching EBM Skills to Medical Students			
Year	Topic	Method	Facilitators
One	Orientation to library resources	Large-group lecture	Librarian
	Searching PubMed	Self-paced web tutorial and quiz Team-based learning session	Librarian
Two	Answering clinical questions	Large-group interactive lecture/small group exercises	Faculty and librarian
	Introduction to EBM—critically appraising a therapy study	Large-group interactive lecture/small-group exercises	Faculty and librarian
	EBM review and Clinical Performance Examination (CPX)	Review small-group hands-on session; assignment and 25-minute individual report back session with a librarian as part of CPX for general medicine	Faculty and librarian
Three	EBM course	Large-group interactive lecture/small group exercises; six-week course	Faculty and librarian
	EndNote	Large-group lecture; individual consults	Librarian
Four	Capstone	Several large-group interactive lectures on therapy and diagnosis	Faculty

EBP requires that clinicians have the skills and resources to conduct clinical research to help inform patient care. Medical schools are strongly urged to ensure that their students graduate with these skills. The skills are best taught in integrated courses that provide instruction and guidance at the point of need, when the learners have the urgency and opportunity to utilize these skills. Librarians, as experts in information management, play an important role in coordinating and conducting training sessions that foster EBP.

NOTES

1. Sackett DL, Rosenberg WM, Gray JA, Haynes RB, Richardson WS. Evidence based medicine: What it is and what it isn't. *Br Med J.* Jan 13, 1996;312(7023):71–72.

2. Sackett DL. Evidence-based medicine. *Semin Perinatol.* Feb 1997;21(1):3–5.

3. National Center for Biotechnology Information, U.S. National Library of Medicine. Evidence-Based Practice. http://www.ncbi.nlm.nih.gov/mesh/68055317. Published 2009. Accessed July 3, 2014.

4. Straus SE. (2005). *Evidence-Based Medicine: How to Practice and Teach EBM.* 3rd ed. Edinburgh; New York, NY: Elsevier/Churchill Livingstone.

5. Richardson WS, Wilson MC, Nishikawa J, Hayward RS. The well-built clinical question: A key to evidence-based decisions. *ACP J Club.* Nov–Dec 1995;123(3):A12–A3.

6. Patel MR, Schardt CM, Sanders LL, Keitz SA. Randomized trial for answers to clinical questions: Evaluating a pre-appraised versus a MEDLINE search protocol. *J Med Libr Assoc.* Oct 2006;94(4):382–387.

7. Straus SE. 3.

8. American Association of Medical Colleges. Report 1: Learning Objectives for Medical Student Education. 1998. https://members.aamc.org/eweb/upload/Learning%20Objectives%20for%20Medical%20Student%20Educ%20Report%20I.pdf. Accessed April 11, 2014.

9. Ibid.

10. Liaison Committee on Medical Education. The 2015 LCME standards reformatting project for public review and comment. http://www.lcme.org/2015-reformat-project.htm. Access April 11, 2014.

11. Ahmadi N, McKenzie ME, Maclean A, Brown CJ, Mastracci T, McLeod RS, Evidence-Based Reviews in Surgery Steering Group. Teaching evidence-based medicine to surgery residents—is journal club the best format? A systematic review of the literature. *J Surg Educ.* Jan–Feb 2012;69(1):91–100.

12. Hadley J, Kulier R, Zamora J, et al. Effectiveness of an e-learning course in evidence-based medicine for foundation (internship) training. *J R Soc Med.* Jul 2010;103(7):288–294.

13. Davis J, Crabb S, Rogers E, Zamora J, Khan K. Computer-based teaching is as good as face-to-face lecture-based teaching of evidence-based medicine: A randomized controlled trial. *Med Teach.* 2008;30(3):302–307.

14. Morley SK, Hendrix IC. "Information Survival Skills": A medical school elective. *J Med Libr Assoc.* Oct 2012;100(4):297–302.

15. Coomarasamy A, Khan KS. What is the evidence that postgraduate teaching in evidence-based medicine changes anything? A systematic review. *Br Med J.* 2004;329:1017–1021.

16. West CP, Jaeger TM, McDonald FS. Extended evaluation of a longitudinal medical school evidence-based medicine curriculum. *J Gen Intern Med.* Jun 2011;26(6):611–615.

17. Barnett SH, Kaiser S, Morgan LK, et al. An integrated program for evidence-based medicine in medical school. *Mt Sinai J Med.* 2000;67:163–168.

18. Martin BA, Kraus CK, Kim SY. Longitudinal teaching of evidence-based decision making. *Am J Pharm Educ.* Dec 12, 2012;76(10):197.

19. Liabsuetrakul T, Suntharasaj T, Tangtrakulwanich B, Uakritdathikarn T, Pornsawat P. Longitudinal analysis of integrating evidence-based medicine into a medical student curriculum. *Fam Med.* Sep 2009;41(8):585–588.

20. Burrows S, Moore K, Arriaga J, Paulaitis G, Lemkau HL Jr. Developing an "evidence-based medicine and use of the biomedical literature" component as a longitudinal theme of an outcomes-based medical school curriculum: Year 1. *J Med Libr Assoc.* Jan 2003;91(1):34–41.

21. Khan KS, Coomarasamy A. A hierarchy of effective teaching and learning to acquire competence in evidence-based medicine. *BMC Med Educ.* 2006;6:59.

22. Medical Library Association. Competencies for lifelong learning and professional success: The educational policy statement of the Medical Library Association. 2007. http://www.mlanet.org/education/policy/knowledge.html. Published September 2, 2008. Accessed April 11, 2014.

23. Slawson DC, Shaughnessy AF. Teaching evidence-based medicine: Should we be teaching information management instead? *Acad Med.* 2005;80:685–689.

24. Maggio LA, Tannery NH, Chen HC, ten Cate O, O'Brien B. Evidence-based medicine training in undergraduate medical education: a review and critique of the literature published 2006–2011. *Acad Med.* Jul 2013;88(7):1022–1028.

25. Simons MR, Morgan MK, Davidson AS. Time to rethink the role of the library in educating doctors: Driving information literacy in the clinical environment. *J Med Libr Assoc.* Oct 2012;100(4):291–296.

26. MacEachern M, Townsend W, Young K, Rana G. Librarian integration in a four-year medical school curriculum: A timeline. *Med Ref Serv Q.* 2012;31(1):105–114.

27. Aitken EM, Powelson SE, Reaume RD, Ghali WA. Involving clinical librarians at the point of care: Results of a controlled intervention. *Acad Med.* Dec 2011;86(12):1508–1512.

28. Morley SK, Hendrix IC. "Information Survival Skills": A medical school elective. *J Med Libr Assoc.* Oct 2012;100(4):297–302.

15

Creating a Curriculum-Based Library Instruction Plan for Medical Students

Amy E. Blevins

There are multiple situations in which librarians may find themselves creating multisession or longitudinal curriculum-based library instruction programs. Maybe you've been hoping to do just this very thing for a while, or you stepped into the shoes of a librarian who did this before you, or possibly you're finding your motivation from an external force. You might be facing this challenge with years of teaching experience or not. No matter what the situation, this chapter will provide tips and strategies for developing a well-rounded library instruction program that focuses on the use of both information literacy skills and evidence-based practice principles.

Creating a successful evidence-based practice instruction plan hinges on several things: experience with information literacy concepts, familiarity with the foundations and principles behind evidence-based practice, an understanding of the foundational knowledge of medical students when it comes to library and information skills, knowledge of the curriculum being used within the medical school at your institution, and a basic understanding of pedagogy. You also need relationships with course directors, negotiation skills, and a willingness to learn from mistakes and constantly make adjustments to how and what you are teaching.

INFORMATION LITERACY AND OTHER COMPETENCIES

The first thing a library instructor should be familiar with is the set of standards for information literacy that the Association for College and Research Libraries (ACRL) has created. The standards indicate that students should be able to determine when they need information and then be able to locate, evaluate, and synthesize information to answer their question while taking into account the ethical, legal, economic, and social issues surrounding the use of information.[1] These competencies are partially echoed by the Association of American Medical Colleges (AAMC) in their 1998 document, which states that medical students should have knowledge of information resources (such as MEDLINE, text books, diagnostic decision support systems, etc.).

It goes on to say that they also need the ability to retrieve information, using skills such as Boolean operators, and to critically appraise the information with which they are presented.[2] A list of learning objectives can be partially drafted by going through these two information literacy documents. Another useful resource is the Compendium of Library/ Informatics Competencies for the Health Sciences Professions that was put together by Eldredge and associates.[3] This resource includes direct quotes regarding library/informatics competencies by degree program from organizations like the Accreditation Council for Graduate Medical Education and the American Nurses Association. According to an article by Eldredge and associates, this resource might be updated every three to five years.[4] When developing and revising a library instruction plan, it can be useful to refer to the compendium for specific competencies.

EVIDENCE-BASED PRACTICE

The AAMC also states that medical students should be "making decisions based on evidence, when such is available, rather than opinion."[5] Before you can draft a plan for a curriculum-based library instruction program, you need to be aware of the basic principles behind evidence-based practice, which uses clinical expertise, patient values, and the best research evidence to make decisions about patient care. It may be helpful to take some continuing education (CE) courses on evidence-based practice such as Supporting Clinical Care: An Institute in Evidence-Based Practice for Medical Librarians, which is held at Dartmouth College. The Medical Library Association (MLA) offers many other CE opportunities on this topic, some of which are online courses.[6] It is essential to be able to speak to medical educators about evidence-based practice and how library instruction can provide medical students with the tools they need to access evidence-based information. Due to the importance of this topic, chapter 14 "Evidence-Based Medicine and Medical Students" is devoted to providing an overview of the major concepts.

STUDENT KNOWLEDGE
AND INFORMATION-SEEKING BEHAVIOR

When planning instruction, think about the prior knowledge and experience that medical students are bringing to the first semester of medical school. Despite the fact that medical students have at least one bachelor's degree and several years of college experience, many of them are relatively unfamiliar with libraries. If they have been exposed to library instruction or information literacy, they are likely still unfamiliar with health sciences resources. Even so, some students feel that they are already highly experienced searchers due to their prior experiences using the Internet. In particular, students often feel that they do not need MEDLINE instruction. A study reported in 2004 showed that medical students frequently stated they did not need a class on MEDLINE, but a survey done in 2001 and 2002 for medical students and dental students showed that 71%–95% of the students indicated that they had learned something about many of the skills presented in class.[7] All students are different, and skills and attitudes change over time, so you may want to include a way to assess student knowledge during library sessions and modify your lesson plans accordingly. One option is to incorporate questions into lectures and PowerPoint slides when teaching in person that can be used to gauge understanding and test assumptions on student knowledge.

Another consideration that can assist with developing an instruction plan is the information-seeking behavior of the target audience. A recent study done by Boumarafi[8] showed that students preferred print resources over electronic resources. Other studies cited showed students were more likely to consult a textbook or a friend when seeking information, and yet others listed MEDLINE as a primary source of information. Dawes and Sampson conducted a systematic review of 19 studies examining the information-seeking habits of physicians. One study listed meetings as a primary source of information, 13 listed textbooks, 4 listed colleagues, and only one listed electronic resources as the primary source of information. In addition, many barriers to accessing information were discussed, and it was estimated that physicians only seek out information for 30% of the questions that arise in their practice.[9] It is important to take this into consideration because the students you teach will tend to model the behaviors they witness in the clinics and from their physician and resident mentors. Perhaps part of the reason physicians pursue so few questions is because of a lack of familiarity with the resources available to them in addition to a lack of access to resources in general.

When designing a library instruction program, it is essential to talk with students about why they are being taught about different resources and why the information being presented is vital. Remind students that they have access to certain resources no matter where they practice medicine and encourage them to become familiar with the resources they have available to them as students so that they can ask for them when they are practicing physicians.

In addition, you may want to talk with course directors and instructors to see what gaps they have noticed in their students' information and evidence-based practice skills. They will have experience with grading assignments and speaking with students on a level that most librarians cannot attain.

Using information regarding competency standards, information literacy, evidence-based practice, and preexisting information skills of medical students, you should be able to put together a comprehensive list of the skills and knowledge that medical students should have upon graduating. At this point, some of the items on the list will be extremely critical, but others may be optional. You may find it helpful to separate out essential skills (such as the ability to run a keyword search in MEDLINE) from skills that may be less essential at this time (perhaps the ability to create an NCBI—National Center for Biotechnical Information—account for saving searches).

CHOOSING RESOURCES TO PRESENT

The next step is to decide which resources you are going to introduce to the medical students. When you look at their courses and assignments, you will notice that they have varying needs at different points in their education. Typically, first-year medical students will have a lot of background questions that are best answered by secondary sources and textbooks. As the students learn, they will develop more complicated foreground questions that may require primary resources. Not only should students be exposed to the different kinds of resources, but they should be taught when to use them.

As they gain the skills needed to engage in evidence-based practice, they will find it helpful to use resources that provide them with evidence-based information. Many health sciences libraries now have subject guides that list out their evidence-based practice resources.[10,11,12] If your library has not done this yet, start one. The number of resources you choose to expose to students will greatly depend on the amount of time you have to work with the students. In general, you may want to stick to two to three resources per hour of instruction.

At the University of Iowa's Hardin Library, access is provided to more resources than can be covered during the library instruction session so the clinical education librarian worked with the developer of the evidence-based clinical practice lectures to develop a flow chart based on the types of questions that students may have (see figure 15.1). The goal is to expose students to the fact that there are many resources at their disposal and that those resources are sometimes better suited to answering different types of questions.

MEDICAL CURRICULUM

Now that you have an idea of the resources and skills that you plan to cover, you need to figure out how to match up those resources and skills with your medical school curriculum. If you are new to your position or institution, you may want to start off by reviewing the website for your medical school or college. An obvious place for library instruction is with

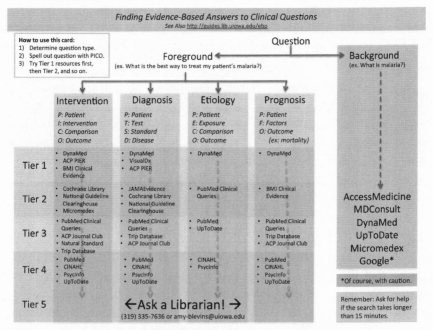

Figure 15.1.   Finding Evidence-Based Answers to Clinical Questions

the evidence-based practice curriculum. Find out when and how evidence-based practice skills are being presented to the students and speak with the people responsible for this instruction. If possible, sit in on the evidence-based practice lectures at your institution. This will help to ensure that your instruction is not in conflict with what the students are learning from other instructors and that the instruction is meaningful for the students.

For example, if the main focus of a course in the curriculum focuses on diagnosis and differential diagnosis, a library instruction session could demonstrate the different filters and subject headings in MEDLINE that can be used to find high-quality articles on diagnostic tests. A brief summary of concepts such as likelihood ratios or sensitivity and specificity can also be worked into the lecture. During the same session, students might also be exposed to textbooks such as *The Patient History: An Evidence-Based Approach to Differential Diagnosis* by Mark C. Henderson and associates. You might also highlight an electronic or mobile resource like VisualDx. If an assignment already exists, you could use the details of the assignment to tailor your lecture to the specific needs of the students. If an assignment does not exist, talk to the course director about developing a project where students are asked to select a diagnostic test for a patient based on evidence regarding the efficacy of the test.

NEGOTIATING

Negotiating for class time can be one of the more challenging aspects of developing a library instruction plan. Work on establishing connections and building relationships before asking for a lot of face time in the curriculum. When speaking to course directors, be prepared to discuss the depth and value of instruction that you can bring to the table as a professional librarian. You might want to refer back to part 1 of this book for further information. Discuss the AAMC and ACRL competencies and talk about the ways in which students can sometimes be overly confident in their ability to find information due to exposure to common Internet search engines. Most importantly, tie your learning objectives back into the learning objectives of a particular course or assignment. You may find that at first, you only see the students once. If that's the case, make the most of that session, and mention the other material that you would cover if you had the time. Sometimes, the students can be the strongest advocates for additional library instruction.

Instruction does not have to happen face-to-face. If you are unable to see the students for more than one session, you can still talk to course directors about posting a news item about library resources in their course management system or linking to tutorials and handouts created by the library. Think of ways that you can maximize the time you do have with students by utilizing in-class activities and promoting active learning. Look into the teaching methods being used by the instructors in the medical school and leverage them for your own endeavors. As demonstrated in part 3 of this book, there are many different ways to present material to your students.

LEARNING FROM MISTAKES (A.K.A. ASSESSMENT)

No one is perfect. There will be times when you present to a class and realize that you forgot to mention an important resource, or the material you chose to cover was too advanced for your students. It's okay.

The important thing is to learn from your mistakes and make the session even better the next time you teach. Talk to your students and learn from your consults. Some of the best teaching examples can come from an impromptu encounter at the reference desk or in the hallway. Talk to your course directors every year and make sure that you understand what they are teaching and what assignments they are asking the students to complete. There are many ways to go about assessment and many things to assess along the way. Look through part 4 of this book for more examples of formal and information evaluations. The important thing is that you never get too comfortable or attached to your lesson plans and that you remember change is constant and practically guaranteed.

BEG, BORROW, AND STEAL (A.K.A. LEARN FROM OTHERS)

You are not alone and you do not need to re-create the wheel. There are numerous articles, posters, and papers on different ways to present MEDLINE, evidence-based practice skills, information literacy, and so on. You can go to a library conference like the annual MLA conference or the local MLA chapter conferences, join a Listserv or a group on Facebook or LinkedIn, and follow librarians on Twitter to learn from your peers firsthand. There are few articles published that specifically discuss curriculum-based library instruction for medical students that takes place throughout their medical education, but there are several librarians talking about their efforts through posters or mentions in other articles.[13,14,15,16]

Every effort should be made to ensure that library instruction is delivered in a way that complements the assignments and information being presented in lectures while building on information literacy skills and competencies. Creating a curriculum-integrated library instruction plan may seem like a daunting task, but it can be done with a little knowledge, some negotiation skills, and the desire to take your teaching to the next level.

NOTES

1. Association of College and Resarch Libraries. *Information Literacy Competency Standards for Higher Education.* 2000. http://www.ala.org/acrl/sites/ala. org.acrl/files/content/standards/standards.pdf. Accessed April 12, 2013.

2. Association of American Medical Colleges. *Report II: Contemporary Issues in Medicine: Medical Informatics and Population Health.* 1998. https://members.aamc.org/eweb/upload/Contemporary%20Issues%20in%20Med%20Medical%20Informatics%20ReportII.pdf. Accessed June 19, 2013.

3. Eldredge JD, Morley SK, Hendrix IC, Carr RD, Bengtson J. Compendium of library/informatics competencies for the health sciences professions. University of New Mexico website. https://repository.unm.edu/handle/1928/15363. 2011. Accessed June 19, 2013.

4. Eldredge JD, Morley SK, Hendrix IC, Carr RD, Bengtson J. Library and informatics skills competencies statements from major health professional associations. *Med Ref Serv Q.* 2012;31(1):34–44.

5. Association of American Medical Colleges. 2.

6. Medical Library Association. Continuing education. http://www.mlanet.org/education/. 2013. Accessed June 19, 2013.

7. Lawrence JC, Levy LS. Comparing the self-described searching knowledge of first-year medical and dental students before and after a MEDLINE class. *Med Ref Serv Q.* Spring 2004;23(1):73–81.

8. Boumarafi B. Electronic resources at the University of Sharjah medical library: An investigation of students' information-seeking behavior. *Med Ref Serv Q.* Oct 2010;29(4):349–362.

9. Dawes M, Sampson U. Knowledge management in clinical practice: a systematic review of information-seeking behavior in physicians. *Int J Med Inform.* Aug 2003;71(1):9–15.

10. Schardt C. Evidence-based practice. Duke University website. http://guides.mclibrary.duke.edu/ebm. 2013. Accessed June 19, 2013.

11. Blevins A, Wallace S. Evidence-based practice. University of Iowa Libraries website. http://guides.lib.uiowa.edu/ebp. 2013. Accessed June 19, 2013.

12. Health Sciences Library. Evidence-based health care (EBHC). University of Colorado website. http://hslibraryguides.ucdenver.edu/ebhc. Accessed June 19, 2013.

13. Eldredge JD. 4.

14. MacEachern M, Townsend W, Young K, Rana G. Librarian integration in a four-year medical school curriculum: A timeline. *Med Ref Serv. Q.* 2012;31(1):105–114.

15. Blevins A. Building evidence-based practice skills in medical students with a four-year curriculum integrated plan. Paper presented at 2013 Annual Meeting of the Medical Library Association, May 3–8, 2013; Boston, MA.

16. McEwen HA, Johnson R, Stockton LM, et al. Evidence-based medicine integration into medicine curriculum. Paper presented at 2013 Annual Meeting of the Medical Library Association, May 3–8, 2013; Boston, MA.

16

Librarians' Role in Evidence-Based Medicine Integration into the Medical Curriculum

Heather A. McEwen, Rienne Johnson, LuAnne M. Stockton, Janice M. Spalding, David M. Sperling, and Lisa N. Weiss

Northeast Ohio Medical University (NEOMED) educates future physicians, pharmacists, and biomedical researchers, including 539 medical students in the 2013–2014 academic year. Effective health care providers need to be able to find relevant information quickly and to assess the relevance and validity of the biomedical literature critically in order to provide the best patient care. Evidence-based medicine (EBM) is a curricular area that provides opportunities for collaboration among librarians and faculty. Librarians at NEOMED have worked with College of Medicine faculty members to integrate EBM longitudinally into the curriculum.[1] Librarian impact can be seen in the enhancement of the EBM curriculum through all four years of medical school. Librarian collaboration with faculty can take multiple forms, and we have learned that success in one area can lead to opportunities in other areas.

Librarians have played multiple roles in the curriculum including teaching, providing access to library resources, assisting with curriculum development, and coaching individual students (see table 16.1). This case study highlights examples of librarian collaboration with faculty members to enhance the education of medical students.

TEACHING

Librarian teaching is integrated into the first, third and fourth years of the curriculum (table 16.2). Librarian participation can involve participating

Table 16.1.   Themes of Librarian Involvement

Teaching	Librarians teach in courses in the curriculum and serve as evaluators for student presentations and projects.
Library Resources	Librarians link students to information resources by creating library tutorials, embedding links within the course management system, and creating library guides focused on curricular topics or courses.
Curriculum Development	Librarians participate in course management by organizing curricular information and participating with curriculum committees.
Coaching	Librarians help individual students with literature searches, proper citation of resources and literature evaluation.

in the management of courses, giving individual lectures, collaborating on assignments with faculty or acting as evaluators for student presentations. A librarian now serves as the course director for the Evidence-Based Medicine I (EBM I) course and as an assistant course director for the EBM II course. Both courses are required for first-year medical and pharmacy students. A second librarian also acts as a faculty member in the EBM I course. Librarians provide lectures and training on subjects ranging from use of PubMed and understanding plagiarism, to conducting systematic reviews. Embedding this instruction in a course, rather than relying on library guides, has allowed for greater interaction between librarians and students, as well as greater support for students as they grow to understand and apply these concepts.

A librarian helps with the creation and grading of assignments, including a short-answer clinical and drug information assignment (see appendix to this chapter). A librarian is also one of the graders for an EBM literature review assignment. Organizing journal club article selection and clinical question assignments is also handled by librarians in the first year of the medical curriculum.

All third-year medical students on their Family Medicine Clerkship complete a Practice-Based Learning and Improvement project that incorporates skills of EBM, critical thinking, and formal presentations. A librarian co-teaches an introductory lecture about the assignment prior to clerkships. The project requires students to develop a clinical question using the PICO format based on a patient encounter, conduct a search of the clinical literature, evaluate the relevance and validity of the article

Table 16.2. Library Instructional Sessions within the College of Medicine

Students	Course	Session Title	Description
M1	Evidence-Based Medicine I	Tertiary Resources Lecture	Instructor: Heather McEwen This lecture introduces students to locating and evaluating print and digital tertiary resources.
M1	Evidence-Based Medicine I	PubMed Lecture and Hands-On Training Session	Instructors: Rienne Johnson and Heather McEwen This session provides students with basic PubMed instruction using online tutorials. The whole class session is focused on advanced training and having students practice searching PubMed.
M1	Evidence-Based Medicine I	Literature Evaluation Lecture	Instructor: Heather McEwen This lecture is focused on the evaluation of journal articles.
M1	Evidence-Based Medicine I	Systematic Reviews and Meta-Analyses Lecture	Instructor: Heather McEwen This lecture discusses how to read and evaluate systematic reviews and meta-analyses.
M1	Evidence-Based Medicine I	Information Mastery and Evidence-Based Medicine Resources Lecture	Instructor: Heather McEwen This lecture discusses online resources, evaluating online resources available, information mastery, and evidence-based medicine-specific resources.
M3	Boot Camp	Practice-Based Learning and Improvement Lecture	Instructors: LuAnne Stockton and Heather McEwen This lecture prepares third-year students for their Practice-Based Learning and Improvement assignments in each clerkship rotation.
M3	Boot Camp	Practice-Based Learning and Improvement Assignment	Evaluators: Librarians Librarians have served as one of three or more evaluators for student group presentations.
M3	Family Medicine Clerkship Rotations	Practice-Based Learning and Improvement Assignment	Evaluators: Librarians Librarians periodically have served as one of three or more evaluators for individual student presentations each rotation.

or guideline they choose as best answering their question, and critically assess and state what answers/recommendations would be provided to that patient and future patients based on the evidence. For the Family Medicine Clerkship, all students on each cycle make formal 10–12 minute presentations of their project to the group as a whole, which are evaluated by peers and faculty, including librarians. Librarian contributions include providing students with suggestions on how to enhance their literature searching as well as on the critical assessment of the article.

Fourth-year medical students have the option to take a research elective in family medicine. When developing their project, students have a two-hour session with a reference librarian to learn how to conduct more advanced searches, how to search for background information, and how to present the information in a project proposal.

LIBRARY RESOURCES

Librarians support faculty and students by providing library tutorials and embedding direct links to articles and resources within the university's course management system (CMS). Course and assignment-specific guides provide curricular resources that are available 24 hours a day. An example of a course-related guide is the EBM I course guide, available at http://libraryguides.neomed.edu/EBM_I_Course. The guide houses links to library resources, resources used in classroom activities, and resources for assignments. From July 2012 to June 2013, the guide was visited 4,482 times. The Citing Resources guide is an example of an assignment-related guide, available at http://libraryguides.neomed.edu/citing. This guide was visited 10,797 times in that same 12-month period. Students use this guide when writing their literature review assignment for the EBM I course as well as for assignments in other courses. Links to relevant guides have been placed in the CMS to provide greater accessibility to students.

In addition to classroom teaching, the library has also created online tutorials on basic PubMed searching and avoiding plagiarism to address specific needs in the EBM courses. Links to these tutorials have been placed in both the library guides and CMS. The tutorials have been placed on YouTube so we can monitor overall usage of the guides.

Librarians also collaborate with faculty to curate and support course or project sites within the CMS. At the request of faculty, an EBM resources site is available to all NEOMED students and is designed to be a resource in the CMS after students have completed their EBM courses. It houses links to EBM-related library guides, websites, and tutorials. It also provides access to EBM-related lecture videos by NEOMED faculty. The site has had 1,440 visits from July 1, 2012, to November 21, 2013.

CURRICULUM COMMITTEES

Librarians serve on curriculum committees and committees focused on educational topics. Educational opportunities have been identified because of librarian involvement in these groups. A potential area of involvement at NEOMED would be librarians serving on curriculum committees for all colleges and collaborating with faculty on research to inform the curriculum as well as enhancement of ongoing initiatives.

Assessment

Assessment of librarian impact on the EBM curriculum has been both quantitative and qualitative. Course and faculty evaluations reveal a positive response by students. Usage statistics allow librarians to have quantitative evidence of the impact of guides and tutorials. Faculty and course evaluations provide feedback about the effectiveness of librarian involvement within the curriculum. Student learning can be evaluated by library-related assignments within the curriculum. These assignments provide feedback to students on their effectiveness in finding information and evaluating information. They can also provide insight to librarians about areas that students are having difficulty mastering. Librarians also actively ask for formative feedback from faculty and students about their educational initiatives. Librarians can have formal meetings or informal hallway discussions with faculty and students about curricular sessions or assignments. This feedback also allows improvement of services and ideas for new tutorials and guides.

CONCLUSION

Faculty and librarians at NEOMED work together to integrate EBM effectively within the College of Medicine curriculum and to develop future physicians who are lifelong learners. There are numerous routes that are available to librarians to make an impact on the curriculum at their home institutions. Faculty and librarian collaboration can effectively integrate EBM within the curriculum to facilitate learners becoming critical thinkers and lifelong learners. Librarians can use the NEOMED examples as possible ways to increase collaboration with faculty members and further the presence of librarians within the curriculum.

APPENDIX

Tertiary Resources Assignment

Examples of questions from the tertiary resources assignment given to first-year students in the Evidence-Based Medicine I course. Please note that drugs, symptoms, diseases, and so on, can be changed to create

Table 16.3. Tertiary Resources Assignment

1. Name a drug that interacts with this herb: noni.   (1 point)

Answer:

Reference:

2. Give two possible differential diagnoses for the following symptom: hypernatremia.
   (2 points)

Answer:

Reference:

3. What is the drug of choice for treating an infection caused by Treponema pallidum?
   (2 points)

Answer:

Reference:

multiple versions of the assignment. The purpose of the assignment is for students to practice using multiple resources to find answers to basic clinical questions. Students are also expected to cite those resources. William McEwen, MLIS, helped with the formatting of the assignment, creation of multiple versions of the assignment, and formatting of the answer database.

NOTES

1. McEwen HA, Johnson R, Stockton L, et al. Evidence-based medicine integration into medicine curriculum. Poster presented at 2013 Annual Meeting of the Medical Library Association, May 2014; Boston, MA. Available at http://lgdata.s3-website-us-east-1.amazonaws.com/docs/1949/769765/EBM_poster_final_-_compressed.pdf. Accessed April 14, 2014.

17

Reflections on Involvement in a Graduate Nursing Curriculum

Jennifer Deberg

The ideal for many instruction librarians, including nursing specialist librarians, is to become as embedded in the curriculum as possible. Although the goals for curricular inclusion can be difficult to achieve in any subject area, it may be more likely to locate collaborators in the nursing and allied health fields due to the team-oriented nature of these professions. In addition, potential areas of information literacy instruction for nursing and allied health students are plentiful. Common objectives might include identifying appropriate sources of evidence for clinical decision making, using flexible and critical thinking skills for building and modifying search strategies, organizing and making sense of evidence, and reporting/formatting sources. I have experienced variable success with integrating instruction in the undergraduate curriculum at my institution, but have identified several opportunities to expand library instruction in the graduate programs. The case study that follows will detail my participation in a clinical doctoral nursing program, including accomplishments, challenges, and ideas for future improvements.

BACKGROUND

Hardin Library for the Health Sciences, part of the University of Iowa Library system, serves all of the health colleges and the neighboring teaching hospital. In 2005, a liaison program was established to provide subject-specific outreach and instruction to all health colleges and departments of the hospital. However, long before the existence of the liaison program, Hardin librarians provided customized service to nursing staff/faculty at the college and the hospital. When I began my work as nursing liaison in 2009, a solid foundation was in place, with a history of regular instruction in most programs at the college level, and strong relationships with many faculty and staff. Librarians had been serving on nursing curricular and hospital committees for some time, further stimulating opportunities for involvement. It is important to mention that the work of key evidence-based practice leaders at the hospital in collaboration with the college had produced the Iowa Model of Evidence-Based Practice in 1994.[1] This model continues to be a driving force for librarian participation in both clinical activities and nursing education.

In 2010, the University of Iowa College of Nursing launched the Doctorate of Nursing Practice (DNP) program. This advanced clinical program prepares practitioners for varying degrees of autonomous practice in increasingly complex practice settings, and is viewed as important for developing nurse leaders who can enhance outcomes and health care quality, fulfill needs for underserved populations, and serve in faculty roles.[2] One of the eight essential components of DNP programs, as outlined by the American Association of Colleges of Nursing, is to promote clinical scholarship and analytical models of evidence-based practice.[3]

DEVELOPMENT OF COURSE-INTEGRATED INSTRUCTION

In early 2010, library orientations for all graduate degree programs were occurring consistently. In-depth library instruction took place primarily in the PhD program and sporadically in the MSN (Master of Science in Nursing) program. The librarian was approached by nursing faculty who had been teaching a course in the MSN program that would be a requirement for DNP students in the adult gerontology and family plans of study. Although the University of Iowa DNP curriculum offers preparation for seven areas of practice, a significant number of students opt for adult gerontology or family plans of study. Interested in better preparing primary care practitioners for evidence-based practice, the instructor for the Primary Care and Older Adult II course proposed an evidence-based practice assignment, including a lecture followed by required consultations with the librarian. Content of the lecture focused on teaching in the following areas: structuring clinical questions, identifying types and domains of clinical questions, evaluating evidence strength, and utilizing clinical and literature databases. Due to a mix of distance and traditional students, the lecture was delivered on-site to most students, but was also recorded and uploaded to the course management site. Individual meetings over the phone, e-mail, or web were conducted with all students, due to a requirement for incorporation of librarian feedback into the assignment. The final product is a presentation in a grand rounds style, with an accompanying written report and handout.

Later in 2010, another opportunity to expand instruction became apparent. The nursing faculty had inquired about locating existing web-based tutorials for evidence-based nursing to supplement a course in development, Evaluating Evidence for Practice. Later, it was learned that the faculty were considering creating a literature review assignment, an ideal chance for library instruction. After several meetings, an assignment was established, including elements recommended by the librarian. The Finding Evidence for Practice course, required for all DNP and MSN students, occurs early in the curriculum, though exact timing varies with area of study. The assignment, a PICO paper followed by a "modified" systematic review, aimed to prepare students to conduct and report a thorough literature search for high-quality evidence. Due to a large number of distance students enrolled in this course, online lectures were created and uploaded by the primary instructor to the course management system. The criteria for the final paper, quite specific and rigorous, were based on internationally known guidelines for conducting and reporting systematic reviews for publication. Since this is a challenging task for most all students, extensive opportunities for individual library instruction have occurred.

CURRENT STATUS AND CHALLENGES

At present, both assignments continue in the courses as described previously (see table 17.1 for more detail.) It is clear that many opportunities for library instruction exist in the DNP program, in order to build

Table 17.1.   Review of Courses

DNP	MSN	PhD
On-site orientation	On-site orientation	On-site orientation
Evaluating Evidence for Practice (Literature Review assignment): Required for all DNP students, regardless of practice area. Taken during first four semesters, though exact timing variable with plan of study.	*Evaluating Evidence for Practice* (Literature Review assignment): taken during second semester of program	*Designing Research*: Course includes extensive library instruction, taken during first three semesters (BSN->PhD or MSN->PhD)
Primary Care and Older Adult II (Evidence-Based Practice assignment): Family and adult/gerontology areas only. Taken in second half of program, simultaneously with clinical rotations.		
Psychiatric/Mental Health Nursing Theory II (Evidence-Based Practice assignment): Psychiatric area of study only		

evidence-based practice capacities. In fact, a recent change expanded the evidence-based practice assignment into another course, Mental Health Nursing Theory II, a required course for DNP students in the mental health plan of study.

For both assignments highlighted in this case study, assessment of learning outcomes has been inconsistent and not nearly as thorough as I would desire. While working on the evidence-based practice assignment (Primary Care and the Older Adult II), students generally report to the librarian or faculty that they have gained knowledge about conducting a search for evidence and incorporating it into a clinical context. However, in 2011 a pre-/posttest revealed increased levels of confidence without improved knowledge. Although I am named "facilitator" of this assignment, I have little participation in grading. As a result, there seem to be missed opportunities for regular assessment of learning. Informal observations and conversations during consultations, combined with a thorough review of submitted papers in the course management system, have indicated that many students have scattered foundation information literacy skills. Assessment has also been sporadic during the PICO paper/modified systematic review assignment (Finding Evidence for Practice). In this course, the librarian does not participate in grading and also lacks access to the course management system. The primary instructor reports high levels of student success with completion of the assignment, which she attributes to library instruction, but this cannot be confirmed.

Another ongoing challenge is to meet the needs of students who are taking courses remotely. For both assignments, lectures and database demonstrations along with other supplemental resources are made available on the course management sites. Although these resources have been modified on several occasions in an effort to better meet the needs of students, the videos often rarely serve as a replacement for individual instruction. Phone and e-mail consultations have been numerous. Web-based consultations have been offered but are not often utilized. The librarian has made regular use of Jing/SnagIt for creating customized demonstrations based on the student topic/needs, with a recent survey indicating that these are highly valued. Finally, volume of work has been a recurring problem at several points in the semester; fortunately, assistance is available from colleagues at the Hardin Library.

FUTURE PLANS

I am working to continue adding value to the curriculum, to ensure sustained participation and impact on student information literacy skills. However, faculty turnover and curricular changes are always a possibility. A pre-/post-assessment of the evidence-based practice assignment is in process for this semester. There are no plans at present to assess outcomes of the PICO paper/modified systematic review assignment, primarily due to lack of faculty interest. Efficacy of instruction has been informally assessed by conversation with students and feedback surveys. This method will continue to be utilized, as it yields information used to modify content and methods of instruction. I plan to work toward broadening the assessment of information literacy skills at appropriate points in the DNP program. An interim DNP program director has indicated receptiveness to having a discussion about this in the future. It is expected that a more comprehensive assessment would be informative for all involved, and should guide future priorities for information literacy instruction.

CONCLUSION

Successful involvement in this DNP curriculum is due to the following factors: a history of well-established faculty relationships, the librarian's opportunistic approach, and a collaborative nursing faculty who are committed to preparing practitioners for evidence-based practice. Although the impact of librarian instruction on student learning is not yet fully known at this institution, the participation described is considered progress toward integration in the curriculum. Of most importance to me is the exposure to librarians as engaged teachers and potential partners.

NOTES

1. Titler M, Kleiber C, Buckwalter K, et al. Infusing research into practice to promote quality care. *Nurs Res.* 43(5):307–313.

2. American Association of Colleges of Nursing. DNP fact sheet. http://www. aacn.nche.edu/media-relations/fact-sheets/dnp. Published January 2014. Accessed March 2014.

3. American Association of Colleges of Nursing. *The Essentials of Doctoral Education for Advanced Practice Nursing.* http://www.aacn.nche.edu/publications/position/DNPEssentials.pdf. Published October 2006. Accessed March 2014

18

Strategies for Building an Information Skills Curriculum: The University of Michigan Experience

Mark P. MacEachern and Whitney Townsend

Librarians at the University of Michigan's Taubman Health Sciences Library interact with all medical students in the classroom consistently throughout the four-year medical school curriculum. As we have described previously,[1] the core sessions of this evidence-based medicine (EBM) curriculum—which is how these sessions are described locally—are scheduled at key points in the students' learning cycle. During the first two years of training, when the students are building their foundational knowledge, we have traditionally focused much of our instruction on background resources (e.g., textbook platforms) and PubMed. As the students' responsibilities shift to clinical work in the third year, we begin to more intensely spotlight evidence-based clinical resources, such as clinical guidelines, systematic reviews, and DynaMed. Each session in this curriculum builds off the one previous, so the students' learning is incremental and progressive. While this approach remains fundamentally intact at present, we have started to shift clinical resources to earlier instruction sessions in response to student feedback and the overall evolution of the medical school curriculum. Our current points of instructional integration are

- Regular instruction sessions (M1–M4) as part of the school's longitudinal EBM curriculum
- Instruction sessions on information retrieval and appraisal in several clerkship rotations

- Small group instruction throughout a family-centered experience longitudinal case series
- Elective sessions for M2 students

The extent to which we are involved in the curriculum is constantly changing. The core educational interventions are more or less fixed, though the structure and content changes over time. We also periodically add sessions and courses at various points to supplement the core EBM training that all students receive. Ultimately, our goal is to facilitate student learning and provide students with the skills to efficiently acquire, appraise, apply, and manage information in clinical practice and biomedical research. In this chapter, we outline the strategies we have used and continue to use successfully to fully integrate an information skills curriculum into our university's undergraduate medical education program.

GOALS AND COMPETENCIES

One of our most important strategies is to proactively identify the local goals, competencies, and philosophies that underlie the curriculum and resonate with key educators and administrators. In our environment, the skills to access and critically evaluate the literature are present within institutional and problem-based-learning competencies.[2] In addition, lifelong learning is highly emphasized in both specific competencies and the overarching philosophy of the curriculum.[3,4] Empowered with this information, we are able to communicate with key curriculum personnel in their own language, using their competencies to support and justify our potential contributions to student learning and the development of the highest quality medical professionals. Because we are able to clearly demonstrate the competencies addressed through our information skills curriculum, medical school administration used a document we created outlining our curriculum-integrated sessions as part of a recent accreditation.

Knowing the fundamental purpose of the curriculum helps us understand the context of our involvement. As simple as that may seem, we think that this understanding is important and worth mentioning. Our instruction is a part of a large, complex organism and should not be viewed—or treated—as one-off, isolated sessions, divorced from everything else that occurs in the curriculum. The skills we help the students develop translate into other aspects of their learning and clinical work. In fact, the sessions we teach are a part of the EBM and medical decision-making components that thread their way through the first two years of the curriculum and clerkship seminars in the later years. With this level of instruction integration, we are able to align our sessions seamlessly with the rest of the EBM curriculum, leading students to perceive efficient search and appraisal as part of the complete EBM process.

RELATIONSHIP BUILDING

In order to integrate successfully into a medical curriculum, we have found that it is imperative to build and cultivate strong partnerships with medical educators. The first step is to identify (or create) faculty champions, those educators who value and support your skills and recognize the potential contributions you can make to the curriculum. Locally, we have had great success building relationships with key stakeholders in medical education, including an associate dean, department chairs, program directors, clinical faculty who teach clerkships and other specialty components, and staff involved in education and student success.

Being proactive in pursuing and developing these connections is vitally important because we cannot expect relationships to develop serendipitously; we cannot expect faculty to come to us, even if they sometimes do. Even those connections who seek us out usually do so because they have heard of our successful collaborations with their colleagues (which more than likely arose because of our being proactive). We present posters and papers at medical education conferences and events, attend faculty meetings, and make a point to integrate ourselves into the local medical education environment. These are all small individual acts, but when combined they go a long way toward creating face and name recognition (our brand) and helping us make inroads with key players.

While we are fortunate to enjoy long-standing partnerships with medical education faculty and administrators, many of our more recent and novel opportunities arose out of relationships with medical education staff. Administrative assistants, educational technologists, and component coordinators all have intimate knowledge of the medical school curriculum and often have the ear of medical education faculty and administrators, making them strong advocates for integration at points that maximize student benefit. Through these connections, we have co-created a second-year elective course on mobile resources, become more involved in third- and fourth-year seminars and online lectures, been offered opportunities to meet with clerkship directors, and developed a standardized presence within the medical school's course management sites. These are all outcomes of collaborations first brainstormed with medical education staff during our daily, more mundane activities, such as scheduling, technology troubleshooting, and even printing out a life-sized poster of a faculty member on the library's poster printer.

COMMUNICATION

To build such relationships we make a point to articulate the importance of information skills within the context of student learning, and how these skills contribute to the school's mission of producing leaders in medicine. In conversations with medical education faculty we focus on student learning outcomes, emphasizing *their* needs instead of the needs or preferences of the library. Perhaps the best example of this approach is our willingness to propose team-teaching sessions with medical educators. In the traditional one-off "library lecture," the key EBM skills that we teach are isolated from the rest of that process. By planning and teaching all of our sessions with medical education faculty and staff, we are able to better connect "library" skills with the evidence-based processes integral to clinical care. Students reap the benefits of this approach because they see an interdisciplinary team of information professionals and medical professionals working collaboratively to solve complex clinical problems. Furthermore, they engage in the EBM process more thoroughly, because in each session they have the opportunity to search for evidence related to a clinical scenario and then discuss the clinical context of what they found with the medical education faculty. As a byproduct of these collaborations, we are able to educate faculty on advances in information skills and resources and build a high level of professional trust. To collaborate in this manner, it is important be open to change, nonterritorial about information skill components and how they are taught, and above all put the needs of the students first.

EVOLVING INSTRUCTION

The battle for librarian involvement does not end with formal integration into the medical school curriculum, however. As the landscape of medical education changes rapidly to address the constantly shifting world of clinical care and medical research, so do information resources and the necessary information skills. We are constantly tweaking (and sometimes completely overhauling) the content and delivery of our instruction, both in response to and anticipation of this changing environment. Each year we re-plan our curriculum-integrated sessions and embrace student and faculty perspectives as we honestly evaluate and consider the need for change. This approach has led to the library being seen as a change agent, rather than as a group who resists change and fears being left behind by the evolving information landscape.

One area that we are able to address through innovative instruction delivery is the shift in medical education toward accommodating and nurturing self-directed learners and lifelong learning skills. We continually and proactively propose moving to online formats of instruction when feasible and appropriate, being careful to maintain the elements of the courses that resonate strongly with students. This often involves implementing new active learning techniques in the classroom, and "flipping" the classroom model to make lecture materials available asynchronously and at the point of need. The educational technologists and course designers are generally happy to assist in formatting our instruction sessions using the established delivery methods that the medical school employs, which in turn provides us with opportunities to develop new relationships and build our support structure.

BEING POISED FOR OPPORTUNITY

At present, it looks as if medical education is about to undergo significant change. The American Medical Association's "Accelerating Change in

Medical Education" initiative in 2013 marks the beginning of a systematic educational overhaul meant to "align medical student training with the rapidly changing healthcare environment."[5] Eleven institutions have been selected, with the results of their curricular changes expected to shape the future of medical education in the United States. Due to our established relationship with medical educators, librarians are included in the curriculum strategic planning process at our institution. Some elements of this larger curricular reform are already in place, including the introduction of supplemental Paths of Excellence programs that provide additional training and opportunities for students in multidisciplinary topics such as global health and disparities and bioethics. By proactively contacting the lead faculty of these initiatives, and by leveraging our preexisting relationships and instructional work within the larger curriculum, we have already begun to embed information skills components into the foundation of these new programs, establishing a model for potential integration into future paths. This, and our many other partnerships, have been a result of a persistent, proactive, responsive, and student-focused approach to information skills development.

NOTES

1. MacEachern M, Townsend W, Young K, Rana G. Librarian integration in a four-year medical school curriculum: A timeline. *Med Ref Serv Q.* 2012;31(1):105–114.

2. Curriculum Policy Committee, University of Michigan Medical School. *Education at the University of Michigan Medical School.* 2012. http://www.med.umich.edu/lrc/medcurriculum/mep/goalslong.html. Accessed March 11, 2014.

3. Ibid.

4. University of Michigan Medical School. Medical curriculum for the MD degree: Curriculum overview/diagram. http://www.med.umich.edu/lrc/medcurriculum/curriculum/map.html. Accessed March 11, 2014.

5. American Medical Association. Accelerating change in medical education. http://www.ama-assn.org/sub/accelerating-change/overview.shtml. 2013. Accessed March 11, 2014.

19

What Is Biomedical Informatics? An Overview and a Case Study

Carolyn Schubert

The biomedical informatics field provides fascinating results in improving patient outcomes, resource allocation, and communication in health care and research settings; however, biomedical informatics has a long and belabored history in U.S. health care. Early work with computers in medicine began in 1959 with a vision of a medical diagnosis database.[1] More than 40 years later, in 2003, the Institute of Medicine was still justifying the use of information technology as a key educational need for health professionals.[2] Building upon information technology infrastructure, biomedical informatics is an "interdisciplinary field that studies and pursues the effective uses of biomedical data, information, and knowledge for scientific inquiry, problem solving, and decision making, driven by efforts to improve human health."[3] Other subfields exist underneath the broad definition of biomedical informatics, such as nursing informatics, public health informatics, clinical informatics, and consumer informatics. To address these issues, biomedical informatics requires knowledge in a variety of realms such as database design, human-computer interaction, and interface design. Many of these competencies draw directly on the skills and knowledge of librarians and informationists.

Recent government action has also pushed the adoption of information technology in health care settings and the use of informatics for improving care. While electronic health records have existed for decades, the widespread adoption has been hindered for a variety of reasons, such as high start-up costs and training needs. The recent HITECH Act incentivized health administrators and health care providers to adopt electronic health records early through financial rewards; the act also promises financial punishments for non-adoption or late adoption.[4] Rewards are based on meaningful use of the system, starting with proper data entry and concluding with generating patient and system reports.[5] The cycle of data input and extraction allows for documentation and assessment of services as a dynamic learning cycle. The act also required the growth of a workforce development program to help develop curricula to train future health IT workers. This expansion of health IT and informatics curricula to allied health workers created an opportunity to explore instruction to other health-focused students.

Biomedical informatics education occurs in a variety of ways. Programs focusing on the information science perspective with some supplementary study of health topics ranges from community colleges to advanced doctoral programs.[6] Tiered competencies and education for these biomedical informatics experts have been discussed and identified by the International Medical Informatics Association.[7] However, competencies for health care providers in the realm of health informatics are slowly emerging. The Technology Informatics Guiding Education Reform (TIGER) initiative identified nursing competencies and education related to nursing informatics at all levels in the mid-2000s.[8] Librarians naturally fit into the TIGER competencies as one of the three core categories is information literacy. As a more recent example, nutritionists are developing tiered skill levels for biomedical informatics.[9] As the momentum continues to integrate information technology into health care settings, librarians have an opportunity to participate in the definition and education of these informatics competencies.

METHODS

James Madison University (JMU) is a comprehensive, teaching-focused institution. The majority of students are undergraduates and some programs include graduate and professional programs. In the summer of 2011, the assistant director of Rose Library, Stefanie Warlick, and the health sciences and nursing librarian, Carolyn Schubert, were invited to revive the Introduction to Informatics for Healthcare Professionals course.

The previous iteration of the course was team-developed with faculty across the curriculum, with primary course instruction completed by the health and human services librarian.[10,11] While there was precedent for the course on campus, the changes in health care and teaching technology allowed for a complete reconfiguration of the course. The course is not housed under a single department but is an elective course hosted through the Institute for Innovation in Health and Human Services at JMU. Because of the partnership, the course has a primary purpose of supporting interprofessional collaboration and is open to all pre-professional health students. Many of the students are in health-related departments, such as Biology, Kinesiology, and Health Sciences. However, the students represent a diverse population of pre-professional health careers, including physician, dentist, physician assistant, nurse practitioner, and health administration.

To prepare for this new course, several areas of professional development were explored, including a literature review, attendance at professional training opportunities, and discussion with other instructors on and off campus. A diverse approach to reviewing the literature was necessary given the intended students. Certain works established an overview of the biomedical informatics field;[12,13,14] however, only one article met both the criteria of addressing recent changes in health care since 2009 and teaching biomedical informatics to undergraduate (or baccalaureate level) pre-professional students.[15] Also, the MeSH (Medical Subject Headings) term "Education, Medical, Undergraduate" defined itself too broadly as a general term for all coursework completed prior to attainment of the MD.[16] Manual sorting and review of articles found very few that matched the baccalaureate education level of health students. Therefore, review of similar undergraduate baccalaureate nursing literature was the closest way to identify a similar population and its curriculum related to biomedical informatics.[17,18,19] Overall, the literature had some useful information on the general topic, but no case studies directly related to the JMU population.

The National Library of Medicine (NLM) and the National Network of Libraries of Medicine (NN/LM) provided a variety of training opportunities, which helped with learning content and developing a professional network. P. J. Grier from the Southeastern Atlantic NN/LM and Dean Karavite from Children's Hospital of Philadelphia developed the "Informatics for Librarians: Peeling the Onion" workshop. Issues addressed in the one-day workshop include an overview of clinical informatics, the federal government's role in health IT, and segments of health IT such as standard terminologies and information design. The foundation of the course provided a greater understanding of the tools in place to gather data and facilitate the generation of new knowledge. More advanced training through the NLM's Biomedical Informatics fellowship provided an even deeper experience to consider the role of technology in improving patient outcomes, improving workflows and cost, and generating new evidence. Undocumented benefits of the course included the week to focus and reflect on biomedical informatics along with a diverse population of health care providers, IT specialists, and librarians. Both of these options were free resources that contributed to the knowledge base useful for teaching the course.

Learning from peers and a network of experts helped to further refine and develop the course curriculum. Networking with the local and dispersed community served as a dual benefit of learning the information, networking with other experts, and establishing my instruction interest in the field. Consultations with previous faculty in Health Services Administration, Economics, and Nursing contributed to the refinement of course curriculum. Additional discussion with key members from the Mid-Atlantic Chapter of the Medical Library Association led to the exchange of course syllabi for comparison with outside institutions and programs. From these pre-planning activities, Warlick and Schubert developed a general course syllabus and course objectives. Course objectives addressed 10 main components:

1. Introduction to health informatics
2. Diverse field of health professions
3. Health informatics and the health care setting
4. Codes and standards for communicating
5. Health informatics and the government
6. Health informatics and economics
7. Health informatics and the patient
8. Health informatics and decision making
9. Health informatics and research
10. Health informatics and future trends

The course utilized active learning strategies, pairing lectures or videos outside of class with activities or case-based discussion in class. To assess student learning from the 10 modules, students completed biweekly reflection papers based on required readings and personal experiences. The papers were due prior to class to ensure student preparedness for in-class discussion. Students were divided into two groups to alternate weeks for paper writing. Table 19.1 gives a breakdown of course topics and active learning activities for each topic.

Table 19.1. Course Topics and Matching Activities

Introduction to health informatics	No activity.
Diverse field of health professions	In-class presentation to peers about a preassigned health profession.
Health informatics and the health care setting	Guest lecture from Health Services Administration faculty member. Introduction to live electronic health record (EHR). Students individually create and enter data into patient record, including use of smart forms and drug-drug checker.
Codes and standards for communicating	Use crosswalk tool to compare and contrast information from ICD-9 codes assigned to patient to ICD-10 codes.
Health informatics and the government	Investigate legislative or advocating activities on professional health organization websites (e.g., American Medical Association)
Health informatics and economics	No activity. Guest lecture from Economics faculty member.
Health informatics and the patient	In-class debate regarding if EHRs help or hurt patients and their quality of care.
Health informatics and decision making	Diet and exercise tracking app activity. Particular emphasis on interface design, activity adherence, and content supplied through app and how it impacted individual knowledge or behavior.
Health informatics and research	Participate in online health forum, HealthTap. Track question and response. Evaluate the utility of the information provided.
Health informatics and future trends	Review Pinterest board of telemedicine pins and identify future trends.

OUTCOMES

The first semester the course was taught JMU's Center for Faculty Innovation facilitated an informal Teaching Analysis Poll (TAP). The TAP evaluated faculty and student performance. Results were used for internal development. After the second semester, students were asked to complete an end-of-course survey regarding student perceptions of the course and its contribution to their future. Almost all students identified "codes and standards for communicating" and "health informatics and the patient" as new information learned from this course and not covered in other coursework. All students identified "health informatics and the government" as new information learned. "Codes and standards for communicating," "health informatics and economics," "health informatics and decision making," and "health informatics and research" were all topics that were not previously experienced or learned through a health-related job or internship. "Codes and standards for communicating" and "health informatics and economics" were topics perceived as least useful in their future careers. "Health informatics and the health care setting" and "health informatics and decision making" were topics perceived as most useful in their future careers.

DISCUSSION

The results of the course survey helped identify the unique content of the course in comparison to the larger curriculum and work-related experiences. As an elective course, the content did not fit into an existing curriculum map of contents or topics. The lack of literature present on health informatics education for baccalaureate-allied health students also did not provide a framework of expectations at other campuses. Therefore, the confirmation that new content was introduced to students through the course was useful. The deeper recognition from students about the role of health informatics and the health care setting and decision making confirmed the relevance of the material to their other coursework or career goals. The indication that these junior- and senior-level students had not learned about the relationship between health informatics and the government was surprising. A significant amount of learning also occurs outside the classroom so highlighting learning through jobs and internships was also important.

As for the topics disliked or poorly valued by students, a broader review of the health care environment is necessary to evaluate whether the topic should continue in the course or if new instructional approaches need to be considered. To start, students did not value the role of standardized vocabularies or coding systems, despite their identification of this as new content not previously experienced in other courses or in job or internship opportunities. Based on other literature findings, the need to understand codes and standards for communicating is role dependent, with nurses as the most frequent users of electronic health records and allied health professionals the least frequent.[20] In addition, the financial incentives provided by the government have limited availability only to physicians and nurse practitioners, not most other allied health professionals. Therefore, many allied health programs and clinics do not have a similar incentive to implement electronic health record systems, which may explain the lack of exposure to this information in other courses or work experiences. Other limitations in student perceptions for coding perhaps also stem from a focus on certain coding standards, such as ICD (a code used for medical billing) and *DSM* (used for psychiatric conditions), based on current debates instead of a broader look at other professional codes such as SNOMED CT (multilingual clinical healthcare terminology used for electronic health records) or Nursing Outcomes Classification. Despite the dislike for the topic, understanding the value structured data and standard vocabularies play in improving patient care is important. Early findings suggest that physicians' use of structured data instead of free text dictation of medical findings positively impacts the quality of patient care in the primary care setting.[21] Therefore, the topic will remain a part of the course, but the method of instruction may vary for better outcomes in the future.

Health economics suffers from a similar situation, as tension exists between needing to learn the material and lack of interest to learn the content. One student commented that the topic was the least interesting "only because [the student] finds economics boring." On the other hand, health care providers are expected to understand the health care system, as seen in a recent call for economics and management training for physicians.[22] While past insurance models have focused primarily on reimbursement for the volume of care, recent implementation of the Readmissions Reduction Program from the Affordable Care Act are starting to apply quality measures to reimbursement procedures. The 30-day hospital readmission of a patient is one example Medicare addresses, since "hospital readmissions are sometimes indicators of poor care or missed opportunities to better coordinate care."[23] This trend establishes a new precedent in tying patient outcomes to reimbursement strategies. Therefore, as future health practitioners, students will need to understand the connection between their professional service and their income, with health IT organizing the evidence of those results. Evidence of coursework involving debates and rhetoric may help provide examples of new approaches to teaching this information.[24]

CONCLUSION

Given the overlap between the information science topics and biomedical informatics curricula and competencies, librarians are well positioned to participate in the informatics education of health students. As the health care system continues to evolve and rely more on health IT, undergraduate allied health students need to start learning about biomedical informatics as a means to transform and optimize care. This chapter documents one early effort at providing biomedical informatics instruction in an interprofessional context as taught by a librarian. Student identification of new items learned in the course reinforces how these skills are not necessarily well-integrated into other existing curricula.

Beyond this case study, other resources exist to support librarians looking to provide course instruction on this topic. As part of the HITECH Act, several institutions received grant money to help with the development of health IT curriculum and shareable modules. Role-based competencies and access to online learning modules are available through HealthIT.gov.[25] Continued assessment of student learning through these modules and other activities can start to establish best teaching practices and strategies.

NOTES

1. Ledley RS, Lusted LB. Reasoning foundations of medical diagnosis. *Science.* 1959;130(3366):9–21.

2. Greiner AC, Knebel E, Institute of Medicine, Committee on the Health Professions Education Summit. *Health Professions Education: A Bridge to Quality.* 2003. http://www.iom.edu/Reports/2003/health-professions-education-a-bridge-to-quality.aspx.

3. Kulikowski CA, Shortliffe EH, Currie LM, et al. AMIA board white paper: Definition of biomedical informatics and specification of core competencies for graduate education in the discipline. *J Am Med Inform Assoc.* 2012;19(6):931–938. doi: 10.1136/amiajnl-2012-001053.

4. Stark P. Congressional intent for the HITECH Act. *Am J Manag Care.* 2010;16(12):24–28.

5. Blumenthal D, Tavenner M. The "meaningful use" regulation for electronic health records. *N Engl J Med.* 2010;363(6):501–504.

6. Dalrymple PW, Roderer NK. Education for health information professionals: Perspectives from health informatics in the U.S. *Educ Inf.* 2011;28(1):45–55. doi: 10.3233/EFI-2010-0889.

7. Mantas J, Ammenwerth E, Demiris G, et al. Recommendations of the International Medical Informatics Association (IMIA) on education in biomedical and health informatics. First revision. *Methods Inf Med.* 2010;49(2):105–120.

8. Technology Informatics Guiding Educational Reform. About us. The TIGER Initiative website. http://www.thetigerinitiative.org/about.aspx. Updated 2014. Accessed July 3, 2014.

9. Ayres EJ, Greer-Carney JL, Fatzinger McShane PE, Miller A, Turner P. Nutrition informatics competencies across all levels of practice: A national Delphi study. *J Acad Nutr Diet.* 2012;112(12):2042–2053.

10. McCabe JA. An assignment for building an awareness of the intersection of health literacy and cultural competence skills. *J Med Libr Assoc.* 2006;94(4):458–461.

11. McCabe JA. The librarian as partner in the development of the health care informatics curriculum at James Madison University. In: Connor E, ed. *A Guide to Developing End User Education Programs in Medical Libraries.* New York: Haworth Medical Press; 2005:37–50.

12. Cleveland AD, Cleveland DB. *Health Informatics for Medical Librarians.* New York, NY: Neal-Schuman Publishers; 2009.

13. Ennis LA, Mitchell, N. *The Accidental Health Sciences Librarian.* Medford, NJ: Information Today, Inc; 2010.

14. Dalrymple PW, Roderer NK. Education for health information professionals: Perspectives from health informatics in the U.S. *Educ Inf.* 2011;28(1):45–55.

15. Hart JK, Newton BW, Boone SE. University of Arkansas for medical sciences electronic health record and medical informatics training for undergraduate health professionals. *J Med Libr Assoc.* 2010;98(3):212–216.

16. National Center for Biotechnology Information, U.S. National Library of Medicine. Education, medical, undergraduate. MeSH website. http://www.ncbi. nlm.nih.gov/mesh/68004504. Accessed December 15, 2013.

17. Jones S, Donelle L. Assessment of electronic health record usability with undergraduate nursing students. *Int J Nurs Educ Scholarsh*. 2011;8:24–923X.2123.

18. Borycki EM, Armstrong B, Kushniruk AW. From prototype to production: Lessons learned from the evolution of an EHR educational portal. *AMIA Annu Symp Proc*. 2009;2009:55–59.

19. Bowers AM, Kavanagh J, Gregorich T, Shumway J, Campbell Y, Stafford S. Student nurses and the electronic medical record: A partnership of academia and healthcare. *Comput Inform Nurs*. 2011;29(12):692–697.

20. Warren J, Gu Y, Humphrey G. Usage analysis of a shared care planning system. *AMIA Annu Symp Proc*. 2012;2012:950–959.

21. Linder JA, Schnipper JL, Middleton B. Method of electronic health record documentation and quality of primary care. *J Am Med Inform Assoc*. 2012;19(6):1019–1024.

22. Wu C, Derman P. A call for management and economic training in medical education. *Acad Med*. 2013;88(5):556.

23. Medicare Payment Advisory Commission (MedPAC). Payment policy for inpatient readmissions. In: *Report to the Congress: Promoting Greater Efficiency in Medicare.*2007:103–114. http://www.medpac.gov/documents/jun07_entirereport.pdf. Accessed December 16, 2013.

24. Jha S. Debates, dialectic, and rhetoric: An approach to teaching radiology residents health economics, policy, and advocacy. *Acad Radiol*. 2013;20(6):773–777.

25. Department of Health and Human Services. Health IT competencies and learning resources. HealthIT.gov website. http://www.healthit.gov/providers-professionals/health-it-competencies-and-learning-resources. Accessed April 14, 2014.

VI

**SUBJECT-BASED INSTRUCTION
IN OTHER DISCIPLINES**

20

What Is Information Literacy?

April Cunningham and Allison Carr

Information literacy is a form of critical thinking used when we engage with information while pursuing a line of inquiry. It requires practice in order to form a habit of mind. The Association of College and Research Libraries (ACRL) defines information literacy as: the ability to "recognize when information is needed and have the ability to locate, evaluate, and use effectively the needed information."[1] Carol Kuhlthau eloquently describes its benefits for learners: "Information literacy enables a person's deep thoughtful process of learning from a variety of sources [and] is at the very core of what it is to be educated in the global information environment."[2] Information literacy empowers people to become independent lifelong learners; they are able to address their needs at any stage in their life, and are more prepared to deal with the demands of the workplace and society.[3] Project Information Literacy found that employers need college graduates who can synthesize the information they find and persevere in order to fully explore a problem. These employees also understand that such work is valuable in order to build knowledge and not just to find the right answer.[4] Information literate citizens understand how information is created, which voices are involved in the conversation and conversely which are missing. They can make informed decisions about their health, their family and their community.

Since the inception of the ACRL Information Literacy Competency Standards for Higher Education[5] in 1989, information literacy has been widely adopted and is gaining traction in higher education organizations. The American Association of Colleges & Universities (AAC&U) has included information literacy as a core competency in its Liberal Education and America's Promise (LEAP) initiative, which has been adopted by 340 schools around the country. LEAP is intended to create "an education that intentionally fosters, across multiple fields of study, wide-ranging knowledge of science, cultures, and society; high-level intellectual and practical skills; an active commitment to personal and social responsibility; and the demonstrated ability to apply learning to complex problems and challenges."[6] In addition to LEAP, many accrediting agencies are now requiring students' information literacy outcomes to be assessed and the findings included in accreditation self studies.[7]

Recognizing that information literacy and the other skills that librarians develop in students are part of the bigger picture of student success, ACRL commissioned *The Value of Academic Libraries Report*.[8] In this report, Megan Oakleaf summarized the existing research about the influence of librarians and libraries on student success, reviewed the accountability movement in higher education, and suggested where librarianship needs to dedicate more research to determining high-impact practices that not only improve information literacy outcomes, but also have a positive effect on students' educational experience overall. This attention to the library's role in the larger context of higher education shows that ACRL recognizes that librarians will continue needing to justify the value of libraries. ACRL's efforts are helping librarians stay informed about the educational reforms and public scrutiny that are ushering in disruptive challenges to higher education (such as competence-based degrees, massive open online courses, and new measures of student success).

The accreditation process is a significant engine for initiating educational reforms in colleges and universities. Most recently these reforms have focused on core competencies (also called essential learning) for graduation and have resulted in widespread calls for learning outcomes assessments. In a trend that appears to be growing, regional accrediting agencies, including Middle States Association of Colleges and Schools and the Western Association of Schools and Colleges, are defining the skills expected of all graduates, and they are including information literacy as one of the competencies they expect institutions to teach and measure. These official efforts have received support from private organizations that are concerned with improving higher education in the United States. Part of the LEAP initiative is to promote authentic assessment of student learning by analyzing the skills that students demonstrate when they complete typical college assignments such as research projects.

Although authentic assessment of learning can take many forms, scoring rubrics are most often used because they define the standards of performance that educators expect students to demonstrate and can define these standards of performance for several dimensions of a paper or project. For example, a rubric can define and support the scoring of multiple criteria (such as grammar, clarity, depth of analysis, research/support, etc.) at multiple levels of achievement (such as developing, competent, and advanced). By using rubrics to evaluate what otherwise might appear to be subjective criteria, educators can develop shared conceptions of appropriate student performance and can capture valid, reliable, and comparable data to use in making decisions about how to improve instruction. By collecting comparable data, educators are able to compare scores among students, among courses, and among institutions when they are trying to identify the interventions that influence student achievement.

In 2009, teams of faculty and other experts brought together by the AAC&U finalized the Valid Assessment of Undergraduate Education (VALUE) rubrics, including one for information literacy that has been adapted by colleges and universities across the country.[9] The VALUE rubrics aim to provide support for the type of large-scale assessment required to measure common outcomes. A related initiative by the Lumina Foundation, called the Degree Qualifications Profile, began in 2011.[10] It defines the core competencies that students should be expected to develop by the time they finish an associate's degree, a bachelor's degree, and a master's degree. It includes information literacy as one of the intellectual skills that students must hone by applying it in their majors and to broader problem-solving challenges.

Overall, the current emphasis on competencies that cut across disciplines and that define what it means to be educated puts librarians' work into a position of strength. If faculty and administrators at your institution embrace the value of essential learning outcomes, you are likely to see more demand for instruction that reaches far beyond the typical one-shot that focuses on the way our search tools work. You will see support for deeper collaboration among departments in order to tap into librarians' expertise and apply it to the ongoing challenge of getting students to dig deeper, transfer their learning from one class to another, sustain intellectual effort, and build their capacities for communicating what they have learned. These collaborations will require leadership from librarians as information literacy experts and will take the form of credit courses or multiple, scaffolded sessions over the span of students' programs. Assessments will show that isolated, one-off sessions make little difference for students' information literacy skills and for their overall academic success.[11]

Information literacy is an important set of skills widely adopted by national higher education groups. It has been recognized to have the same level of importance as critical thinking and writing in foundational skills by national accrediting bodies. Information-literate citizens think critically about issues and the information they use when making decisions about their health, job, family, and life.

NOTES

1. American Libraries Association. *Presidential Committee on Information Literacy: Final Report.* January 10, 1989. http://www.ala.org/acrl/publications/whitepapers/presidential. Accessed January 14, 2014.

2. Kuhlthau C. Rethinking the 2000 ACRL Standards. *Comm Info Lit.* 2013;7(2):92–97. http://www.comminfolit.org. Accessed January 10, 2014.

3. Breivik P. *Information Literacy and Lifelong Learning: The Magical Partnership.* http://bivir.uacj.mx/dhi/DoctosNacioInter/INFORMATIONLITERA-CYANDLIFELONGLEARNING.htm. Accessed January 15, 2014.

4. Head A, Van Hoeck M, Eschler J, Fullerton S. What information competencies matter in today's workplace? *Libr Info Res.* 2013;37(114):75–104. http://www.lirgjournal.org.uk/lir/ojs/index.php/lir/article/view/557/593. Accessed January 14, 2014.

5. Association of College and Research Libraries. *Information Literacy Competency Standards for Higher Education.* January 18, 2000. http://www.ala.org/acrl/standards/informationliteracycompetency. Accessed January 10, 2014.

6. Association of American Colleges & Universities. *College Learning for the New Global Century.* 2007. http://www.aacu.org/leap/documents/GlobalCentury_final.pdf. Accessed January 10, 2014.

7. Association of College & Research Libraries. Information literacy and accreditation agencies. http://www.ala.org/acrl/issues/infolit/standards/accred/accreditation. Accessed January 14, 2014.

8. Oakleaf, M, Association of College and Research Libraries. *The Value of Academic Libraries.* September 2010. http://www.ala.org/acrl/sites/ala.org.acrl/files/content/issues/value/val_report.pdf. Accessed January 17, 2014.

9. Association of American Colleges & Universities. *Information Literacy VALUE Rubric.* http://www.aacu.org/value/rubrics/pdf/InformationLiteracy.pdf. Accessed January 17, 2014.

10. Lumina Foundation. *The Degree Qualifications Profile.* http://www.luminafoundation.org/publications/The_Degree_Qualifications_Profile.pdf. Accessed January 17, 2014.

11. Oakleaf M. 8.

21

How to Achieve Information Literacy Integration

Allison Carr and April Cunningham

Librarians can make changes to their instruction programs so that they not only strengthen their own offerings but also influence changes at the institution level as well. Librarians should also be encouraging curricular revisions and institutional assessment initiatives that emphasize information literacy as essential learning in undergraduate, professional, and graduate programs. In this chapter we give examples and describe the facets of making the kinds of changes that can result in significant infusion of information literacy throughout the curriculum.

EXAMPLES

Multi-shot Sessions

Multiple instructions sessions are the natural extension of a one-shot. Frequently, after you have worked with the faculty for a while and they have seen the outcomes of the one-shot session, both of you may identify a need for more in-class time to continue what was started in the initial session. Initiating conversations inquiring about how students are completing the assignments and what faculty see as missing is a great way to identify that more in-class time would benefit students. Multiple instruction sessions can foster deeper integration with the curriculum, allow students more time to process and practice what they've learned, and develop stronger relationships with their librarian. The following case studies will address multiple instruction sessions in more detail.

Embedded in (or Contributed Content to) an Online or Hybrid Course

As more online and hybrid courses are offered, embedding a librarian in the learning management system (LMS) can ensure that students have access to a librarian where they do the most work. This was covered in the chapters on online instruction and blended learning. In some hybrid courses, embedding the librarian in the LMS coupled with face-to-face instructional sessions can be effective.[1] But for distance students, the librarian's presence in the LMS may be the only contact they have with a librarian. Additionally, digital learning objects may be useful in reaching students when a librarian cannot be "present" in an LMS.[2]

Assignment Development

Some successful information literacy integration may never result in instruction sessions. Librarians can be powerful collaborators with faculty to develop classes that cultivate information literacy. Leveraging our wide-ranging experience with different assignments can lead to refreshed and refocused assignments. Faculty-librarian collaboration on assignments is an effective way to ensure that information literacy outcomes are being met in specific courses, without the added commitment to teach a class. This can manifest in one-on-one or group discussions about an assignment or faculty development workshops.[3] This strategy allows librarians and faculty to share the responsibility of teaching information literacy rather than having it live solely in the library.

Team Teaching with Disciplinary Faculty

Team teaching with disciplinary faculty can be a valuable experience for the librarian, faculty, and students. The disciplinary faculty provides the needed content expertise, while the librarian provides expertise in student learning and information literacy. The librarian and disciplinary faculty work together on learning outcomes and assignment and lesson development, and often co-teach the class together.[4,5] The students are more likely to see how the research process is intertwined with their own studies instead of being an isolated piece of their education.

For-Credit Courses

For-credit courses can take many forms, from a one-credit companion course or lab to a three-credit information literacy requirement, and they may be face-to-face, hybrid, or online. Sometimes, the course lives within the library, with the librarian developing the content, exclusively teaching the course and grading the students' work. A primary benefit of semester-long courses is the additional contact time with a librarian. More time to work with students can cultivate a deeper understanding of the research process and information literacy.[6] The librarian sees the product of the students' work, which is not usually the case in one- or multi-shot sessions. Challenges include the amount of time needed to administer the course and the evaluation of students' work, as many librarians are not trained to teach or grade.[7]

Changes to University/Curriculum

Librarians are in a unique position to have a broad view of curriculum at a university, where they can see how the courses and programs are intertwined. Additionally, librarians may also see places where student research currently exists, or could exist. Using this knowledge, along with national movements toward student learning outcomes and assessment, can be useful in making curricular changes. Working within the structure of your university, use the university and general education curriculum committees to your advantage. Use the national push for student learning outcomes and assessment in accreditation to advocate for inclusion in information literacy in the curriculum. As McGuinness describes, an effective way of integrating information literacy in a meaningful way is to go for a top-down approach where information literacy is added to the mission of the university with widespread support from Academic Senate and curriculum committees.[8]

Large-Scale Assessments

Large-scale assessments, often undertaken as part of an institution's accreditation process, involve large samples of students and are intended to measure students' knowledge and skills as they begin or end a program or degree. These assessments involve institutional researchers, teams of faculty, as well as staff and administrators. When librarians are involved in large-scale assessments, they are able to provide expertise in defining information literacy, creating or identifying assessment instruments that will generate useful data about students' information literacy outcomes, and analyzing the results of the assessments to explain what the data suggest about students' learning and what could be changed to improve the outcomes.[9]

SETTING PRIORITIES

We've reviewed some of the forms that curriculum-based instruction can take. In addition, you can read more about librarian roles in chapter 1. Before you start trying to decide which of these methods might work best for you, it's imperative that you first take time to focus on your purpose for considering making changes.[10] The advice in this section is meant to help you to identify and strengthen your own core professional values (the ones that are inspiring you to take a risk and make a change in your instruction) before you bring your ideas forward to your colleagues. Whether the impetus to change comes from outside pressures—whether created by budget cuts, accreditation requirements, the preferences of your supervisor—or your own ambition for recognition, you should first consider your own values before taking action. Also, keep in mind that your ultimate goal is to intensify the influence of your instruction.

Two common mistakes when considering your own professional values are hyper-pragmatism and instrumentalism. Hyper-pragmatism limits you to what is most achievable, rather than what is best, such as administering a satisfaction survey when what you want to know is how much students learned. Instrumentalism leads you to do what is most pleasing to those around you—for instance, being of service to faculty.[11] To avoid both

of these pitfalls, focus instead on your values by asking "Do the consequences of my actions measure up to the values that motivate my work?"
and "What commitment am I willing to make?"[12,13] Finding the answers to
these questions will help you to set your own standards to improve your
instruction.

Priorities at the Program Level

Once you have decided what commitment you're willing to make individually, you'll want to share your transformation with your colleagues in
the library to improve the effectiveness of your actions for students. Make
an effort to tie your new, values-driven plans to the values that inspire
your colleagues' work. Your fellow librarians and your administrators/
supervisors probably share your values for students' learning and success,
even if their actions do not always demonstrate those values. So look at
formal and informal statements of values and motivation coming from
your department, such as mission statements, accreditation self-study reports, annual reports, and job descriptions, for evidence of the principles
that guide your organization. Whether you are seeking input about which
curriculum-based initiatives to pursue or you are announcing the plan
you're going to implement, making explicit appeals to your colleagues'
values will help you to give context to what might otherwise seem like
arbitrary changes if your instruction program appears to be working.

You and your colleagues will also benefit from curriculum mapping
to identify the programs and students your current program is not reaching.[14] Working on a curriculum map can be a great way to see if your
programmatic actions and goals are aligned. This can open the space
for discussing your reasons for wanting to emphasize curriculum-based
instruction. It will also show your colleagues that you will take accountability for using their time wisely and doing your best to make sure that
their new or expanded curriculum-based instruction efforts will move
your program closer to the goals you all share.

Priorities at the Institutional Level

Initiating changes at the institutional level to improve students' information literacy will often require more strategy than it takes to make changes

within your library's program. Look for curriculum-based solutions that may already be in place because they are being led by other campus partners. Or suggest librarian-led projects that augment, rather than replace, existing successful interventions for students. Librarians who have a clear view of their value-based goals are also likely to find, over time, that educational improvement trends (such as the current interest in core competencies and institutional learning outcomes) will create demand for the kinds of support services that librarians are well positioned to provide. Stay alert and play the long game.

If, like most librarians, you are feeling pressure to undertake assessments, make sure what you're assessing is what's most important to you. And use action research, program review, and student learning outcomes assessment to help clarify priorities within your instruction program and at the institutional level. When your work is rooted in your values, the data you gather and the insights you gain from assessment will give you something to share with the people you're trying to influence to make changes. Positioning yourself for this collaboration is the subject of the next section.

POSITION YOURSELF

Collaborating with disciplinary faculty is imperative in order to provide meaningful library and information literacy instruction. With the exception of a few types of instruction (stand-alone workshops, reference interactions), librarians cannot provide quality instruction without working closely with faculty.

Often librarians have to ask faculty for permission, and hope that faculty agree. We must instead behave in such a fashion that illustrates a belief in our professional ideals. Our perspectives on curriculum and assignments are unique, and our understanding of student learning is invaluable. We must carry this confidently in all interactions we have with faculty.

Working with faculty often takes a change in language, but not a change in philosophy. Inquiring about the faculty's goals for their students may be a good way to learn more about how they do research in their own field (and what's expected of students in this regard as well). Information literacy can be a politically loaded or misunderstood term, but that shouldn't deter you. Further, information literacy does not have to be the language that you use when working with faculty. Starting with a conversation about how your faculty's discipline values and practices inquiry is a great opener. Faculty have ideas of what they want their students to learn about how research is conducted and communicated in their discipline, and librarians can provide feedback as to how to help students learn this.

Ivey found four behaviors that are essential for success in collaboration: "a shared, understood goal; mutual respect, tolerance, and trust; competence for the task at hand by each of the partners; and ongoing communication."[15] Often the shared goal is increasing students' understanding and demonstration of a disciplinary line of inquiry. To help the faculty understand your perspective and expertise, develop an elevator speech that is not discipline specific. For example, a short definition of what information-literate students look like and how librarians can help get them there may open a conversation with a faculty member.

In addition to working with the willing and interested faculty members who are open and eager to include information literacy in their courses, institutional change is a very important way to fully integrate information literacy formally into the curriculum.[16] Identifying and cultivating partners who are willing to speak at an institutional level on behalf of librarians can be an effective way to promote information literacy. While librarians can be skilled in advocating for information literacy in curricula, voices beyond the library may carry more weight with decision makers on campus.

WHAT HAPPENS WHEN IT WORKS

When you set priorities that are based on your values and you cultivate connections inside and outside your library, you are well positioned to deal with what happens next. Often, this will result in an increased instruction workload and time commitment and increased number of students asking for assistance at your reference desk. While an exciting prospect for you, you may encounter negative feedback from your colleagues, if they also experience increased workload unexpectedly. Open communication and collaboration with colleagues may be helpful in alleviating or preventing negative reactions.

Unintended consequences of the changes you're implementing won't only happen inside your library. They can also surface at the institution level. As you prepare to try your new ideas, consider the following:

- When faculty offering courses that meet the institution's information literacy requirement are mandated to take students to the library, it can create compliance without commitment and waste everyone's time. Consider focusing your time on allies.
- If you hope your curriculum-based instruction will protect the library from cuts or other threats, you will probably be disappointed when it turns out that your budget is just as threatened as ever. On the other hand, good assessment data from your collaborations might make it possible to ask for small investments from your institution in the form of grants or technology.
- Stand-alone information literacy instruction, even when it's large scale (e.g., a general information literacy course or a required online tutorial), is often invisible to faculty in the disciplines so students often aren't supported in transferring their skills from one setting to another.
- Although core competencies and institutional learning outcomes assessments can be a powerful engine for bringing librarians' interests in student learning to the attention of colleagues outside the library, be prepared for faculty resistance.
- Instruction that focuses on tools will not make a significant change in students' assumptions about research, so keep your instruction focused on processes and concepts. That means you might have to deal with some people (both inside and outside the library) questioning whether what you're teaching is really the librarian's purview.

Overall, if you're successful in growing your instruction program, you will reach a point of saturation and no new collaborations can be squeezed into your schedule. At that point your decisions about when to continue and when to phase out existing instruction relationships to make room for new ones will come down to which disciplines to target, when you believe students can benefit from instruction most, and which unique information literacy skills or concepts each collaboration gives you the opportunity to introduce/reinforce. You may be able to transition some instruction from time-intensive in-person sessions to assignment or learning-object development (i.e., working with faculty to create information literacy assignments that they will deploy in their own courses).

CONCLUSION

When you take control of your transformation you will lead your colleagues inside and outside the library by example.[17] Be motivated by your values and you'll not only be more likely to happen across new opportunities to improve your instruction through collaboration, but you'll also be better prepared to explain the advantages of your approach to the librarians, faculty, and administrators you want to influence. If your primary reaction to the suggestion that you should consider improving your instruction program through curriculum-based instruction is to assume that you will not receive the support and collegiality that this requires, we suggest the book *Learned Optimism* by Martin Seligman.[18] He outlines a research-based technique for challenging negative assumptions and replacing them with optimistic explanations. Often making a change in how you interpret interpersonal frustrations can lead to changes in how you interact with the people you want to influence. And this change in your habits can result in different, and more positive, outcomes.[19]

NOTES

1. Kobzina N. A faculty-librarian partnership: A unique opportunity for course integration. *J Libr Admin.* 2010;50(4):293–314. http://www.tandfonline.com/doi/abs/10.1080/01930821003666965. Accessed January 15, 2014.

2. Jackson P. Integrating information literacy into Blackboard: Building campus partnerships for successful student learning. *J Acad Libr.* 2007;33(4):454–461. http://www.sciencedirect.com/science/article/pii/S0099133307000869. Accessed January 15, 2014.

3. Miller R, O'Donnell E, Pomea N, Rawson J, Shepard R, Thomes C. Library-led faculty workshops: Helping distance educators meet information literacy goals in the online classroom. *J Libr Admin.* 2010;50(7/8):830–856. http://www.tandfonline.com/doi/abs/10.1080/01930826.2010.488977. Accessed January 8, 2014.

4. Schulte S. Integrating information literacy into an online undergraduate nursing informatics course: The librarian's role in the design and teaching of the course. *Med Ref Serv Q.* 2008;27(2):158–172. http://www.tandfonline.com/doi/abs/10.1080/02763860802114272. Accessed January 10, 2014.

5. Pritchard P. The embedded science librarian: Partner in curriculum design and delivery. *J Libr Admin.* 2010;50(4):373–396. http://www.tandfonline.com/doi/abs/10.1080/01930821003667054. Accessed January 8, 2014.

6. Clapp M, Johnson M, Schwieder D, Craig C. Innovation in the academy: Creating an online information literacy course. *J Libr Info Serv Dist Learn.* 2013;7(3):247–263. http://www.tandfonline.com/doi/abs/10.1080/15332 90X.2013.805663. Accessed January 10, 2014.

7. Schulte S. 4.

8. McGuinness C. Exploring strategies for integrated information literacy. *Comm Info Lit.* 2007;1(1):26–38. http://www.comminfolit.org/index.php?journ al=cil&page=article&op=view&path[]=Spring2007AR3. Accessed July 3, 2014.

9. Oakleaf M. Association of College and Research Libraries. *The Value of Academic Libraries.* September 2010. http://www.ala.org/acrl/sites/ala.org.acrl/files/content/issues/value/val_report.pdf. Accessed January 17, 2014

10. Saunders L. Regional accreditation organizations' treatment of information literacy: Definitions, collaboration, and assessment. *J Acad Libr.* 2007;33(3):317–326. http://www.sciencedirect.com/science/article/pii/S0099133307000365. Accessed January 15, 2014.

11. Meulemans Y, Carr A. Not at your service: Building genuine librarian-faculty partnerships. *Ref Serv Rev.* 2013;41(1):80–89. http://dx.doi.org/10.1108/00907321311300893. Accessed January 15, 2014. Accessed January 15, 2014.Ibs t to it.f importance as critical thinking and writing in foundational skills. . .

12. McAteer, M. *Action Research in Education.* London, England: SAGE; 2013.

13. Block, P. *The Answer to How Is Yes: Acting on What Matters.* San Francisco, CA: Berret-Koehler; 2002.

14. Lowe MS, Booth C, Chappell A, Stone SM, Tagge N. *Visual Curriculum Mapping: Charting the Learner Experience.* 2013; Paper 18. http://scholarship.claremont.edu/library_staff/18. Accessed January 17, 2014.

15. Ivey R. Information literacy: How do librarians and academics work in partnership to deliver effective learning programs? *Aust Acad Res Libr.* 2003;34(2):100–113. http://www.tandfonline.com/doi/abs/10.1080/00048623.20 03.10755225. Accessed January 15, 2014.

16. McGuinness C. 8.

17. Block, P. 13.

18. Seligman, M. *Learned Optimism: How to Change Your Mind and Your Life*. New York, NY: Vintage Books; 2006.

19. Quinn BA. Enhancing academic library performance through positive psychology. *J Libr Admin*. 2005;42:79–101. http://www.tandfonline.com/doi/abs/10.1300/J111v42n01_05. Accessed January 15, 2014.

22

A Curricular Approach to Information Literacy Instruction in Sociology: A Case Study

Adam T. Beauchamp

Information literacy instruction in higher education is dominated by one-shot library instruction, and the library literature is full of studies and advice on how to make the best of this one chance to make an impact on student learning. No matter how effective the teaching strategy, though, one session in isolation is not enough to cover the full range of information literacy skills. However, librarians seeking to provide curricular information literacy instruction need not abandon this familiar library instruction format. What follows is an examination of how instruction librarians at Tulane University redeployed the one-shot to provide sustainable and meaningful information literacy instruction to undergraduate sociology majors.

DOING MORE WITH LESS

Providing quality information literacy instruction to the students at Tulane University presents challenges that are likely familiar to academic librarians. First is the problem of limited resources. Howard-Tilton Memorial Library, Tulane's main campus library, enjoys rich collections but ranks low in the number of professional staff when compared to other members of the Association of Research Libraries (ARL).[1] Most reference services, research consultations, and classroom instruction are provided by five librarians on a campus of roughly 8,000 undergraduates, with another six librarians providing only occasional student services outside their other primary duties. Thus, we could not simply increase the total number of sessions offered to achieve curricular information literacy goals.

The solution was to be strategic about when and where information literacy instruction is provided, so the librarians at Howard-Tilton sought out places in the curriculum where a limited number of library instruction sessions could have the highest impact. We examined the undergraduate curriculum to understand its structure, and mapped onto this curriculum the information literacy skills students need to succeed at each stage of their education. Since the undergraduate curriculum at Tulane offers students considerable freedom in their course selection and degree planning, and consequently minimizes common curricular experiences, we focused instead on the undergraduate majors. This brings us to the sociology program at Tulane, our focus for the remainder of the case study.

The sociology major is noteworthy for its prescribed sequence of methodology courses, to be taken early in a student's career. Undergraduates interested in sociology can choose from a variety of introductory courses at first, but then must take three courses in strict succession before moving on to advanced electives. These three courses are Foundations of Sociology (SOCI 2010), Research Design (SOCI 3030), and Research Analysis (SOCI 3040), taken in this order. In the foundations course, students are introduced to the basic concepts and theories of sociology. Next, in Research Design, students learn the methods of social science research. Finally, students in Research Analysis learn quantitative methods and basic statistics. This sequence presented a curricular space in which librarians could reach all sociology students and integrate progressive information literacy instruction.

GAINING ACCESS

The next challenge was to gain access to these targeted courses. Often librarians must lobby faculty members for access to students in their courses; the use of words like *outreach* and *liaison* to describe librarians' relationship to the institution as a whole confirms our otherness and need to initiate connections to the "regular" instructors at the university. This is not to say that librarians are powerless to effect change or influence student learning, but it does require an understanding of the organizational culture of our institutions and a certain skill in navigating this political terrain.[2,3,4] At Howard-Tilton, librarians rely on cultivating personal relationships with teaching faculty in order to provide information literacy instruction to their students.

Essential to our efforts to promote information literacy instruction are the "library fans." These are instructors who already value collaboration with librarians and reliably request a one-shot library session for their classes each semester. When formal alternatives are unavailable, the road to building an information literacy curriculum can begin with these faculty members. The Sociology Department at Tulane includes several library fans, and two in particular proved the most helpful since they taught sections of SOCI 2010, the first of the required three-course sequence. Creating the best possible one-shot session for these instructors not only demonstrated value and developed the instructors' trust in librarians' pedagogical expertise, but created allies for expanding librarians' access to other target courses.

Building on the support of our library fans, we were able to suggest that library sessions become a standard feature of the degree program, emphasizing the desirability that all sociology majors have a common learning experience. Having these faculty members promote library sessions to their colleagues carried more weight than had it come directly from librarians. Buy-in from the faculty did not materialize overnight, but in three semesters' time we had every section of SOCI 2010 participating in library instruction, all using the same annotated bibliography assignment to ensure students learned how to identify and describe sociological scholarship and compile their selections into a coherent bibliography.

At the same time that standardized information literacy instruction gained traction in SOCI 2010, librarians worked with those same professors to discover which research skills were still in need of development in their next course, SOCI 3030. The library session in the first course served as a good foundation, but students fell short when making connections between existing scholarship and their own proposed research. With this in mind, a library session was added to SOCI 3030 that reinforced search techniques but shifted the focus to literature reviews in order to emphasize research as a form of scholarly communication.

The literature review session in SOCI 3030 was successful, and the professors teaching these sections reported improvements in students' understanding in class discussion and on midterm exams. One instructor then sought out further engagement with the library's resources. Her initial request to show students "archival sources" evolved into a very popular library workshop centered not on searching for information, but rather on using common library materials to practice content analysis methods. This kind of activity has been written about in the scholarship on teaching and learning in sociology,[5,6] and we succeeded in adapting it to the library setting. This too became a universal feature of the course, and now all sections of SOCI 3030 include two sessions at the library.

The last course in the sequence, SOCI 3040, has proven the most challenging in the curricular approach to information literacy. The objective of this quantitative methods course is to teach students basic statistical methods, and it does not have a standard research component. However, librarians knew from experience that students often struggle with finding existing data sets to use in statistical assignments. Coincidentally, two new professors were recently hired to teach this course, and at the annual New Faculty Happy Hour hosted by the library, we made sure to meet them and advocate for library instruction. The sales pitch was successful, and we continue to work with these instructors to develop a library session on operationalizing a research question and locating appropriate data sets for secondary analysis.

ASSESSING AND LEARNING

Just as library sessions were added to key sociology courses to progressively enhance students' information skills, assessment techniques served to link the courses together, reinforcing previous learning while creating the scaffolding for more advanced skills and concepts. One such assessment used consistently throughout the program is a homework assignment before each library session.

Before the library session in SOCI 2010, students have to locate an academic article on a topic of interest, explain why they think it is sociological, and bring it to the library session. There are no prompts suggesting where students should search or how they should evaluate results.

This establishes which search tools students are comfortable using and what criteria they already use to evaluate academic work. The assignment promotes metacognition, forcing students to reflect on their current search process, and is then used as a point of comparison to the search tools and techniques taught in the library session.

As with other one-shot sessions, the success of library instruction in SOCI 2010 is measured with formative assessments during class and by the professor through annotated bibliographies due at the end of the term. However, in keeping with our curricular information literacy goals, assessment of SOCI 2010 happens again in homework assigned to students in the next course, SOCI 3030. Again, the assignment is to retrieve and analyze a scholarly article on their topic of choice, and as before, it serves as an assessment of what students already know. This time, however, librarians and professors can compare students' base knowledge to that of the previous semester, and note their application of information literacy skills taught in SOCI 2010. And once again, this homework assignment becomes an instrument for teaching more advanced concepts. This pattern is repeated in the second library session of SOCI 3030 and again for the quantitative methods exercises in SOCI 3040. Thus, each pre-library session assignment reinforces the lessons of earlier library instruction and provides a platform on which to develop new skills, effectively creating a matrix of formative assessments to track students' sequential learning. Librarians are also looking past SOCI 3040 for ways to assess the quality of students' research in their upper-level electives. This will depend on establishing working relationships with instructors of those courses, and will likely depend on the good will and support already in evidence between librarians and the faculty members teaching the three-course sequence in sociology.

CONCLUSION

The curricular approach to information literacy instruction in the sociology major at Tulane University is built upon strategic placement of library sessions, personal relationships with teaching faculty, and a series of interlocking assessments. As a result, the humble one-shot instruction session became a powerful tool to support student learning throughout the sociology curriculum, and could serve as a model for curricular information literacy efforts in other programs on campus. Faced with few options for curricular information literacy campus-wide, and without a strong institutional voice in curricular planning, the librarians of Howard-Tilton take advantage of existing opportunities to create a program of information literacy instruction, one major at time.

NOTES

1. Kyrillidou M, Morris S. *ARL Statistics 2010–2011*. Washington, D.C.: Association of Research Libraries; 2012; p.99. Available at: http://publications.arl.org/ARL-Statistics-2010-2011/.

2. Anthony K. Reconnecting the disconnects: Library outreach to faculty as addressed in the literature. *Coll Undergrad Libr* 2010;17(1):79–92.

3. Christiansen L, Stombler M, Thaxton L. A report on librarian-faculty relations from a sociological perspective. *J Acad Libr* 2004;30(2):116–121.

4. Kotter WR. Bridging the great divide: Improving relations between librarians and classroom faculty. *J Acad Libr* 1999;25(4):294–303.

5. Taylor F. Content analysis and gender stereotypes in children's books. *Teach Sociol* 2003;31(3):300–311.

6. Messinger AM. Teaching content analysis through Harry Potter. *Teach Sociol* 2012;40(4):360–367.

23

Evolution of an Undergraduate Business Information Literacy Class: A Case Study

Kimberly Bloedel

Academic business librarians receive a variety of reference questions from students. Where can I find information on XYZ company? What are the trends in the restaurant industry? How many people live in the zip code 52245? What are the risks of doing business in Brazil? In most cases, business reference questions fall into four broad categories: company information, industry and market information, business climate information (demographic and economic data), and international business information. Accordingly, business reference sources can be divided into those four broad categories. Understanding how business information is organized is very important for business students' success in both academic and career settings. A recent study[1] on information literacy in the workplace revealed that employee decision making depends on knowing how to find information. Participants in the study also stated that their organizations used company and industry information.[2] A class that focuses on how to access and evaluate business information can play an integral role in supporting business students' research process.

Since 1988, the librarians at the University of Iowa Pomerantz Business Library have helped business students develop information literacy skills by offering a one-credit business information research class. Always part of the Tippie College of Business curriculum, the class was first offered to MBA students. Due to curriculum changes in the MBA program in the early 1990s, the class was discontinued. In 1996, the class was offered as a one-credit elective to undergraduate business students. Over the years the undergraduate class has evolved in response to curriculum needs, student needs, and technology advancements. However, the goal has remained the same: to introduce students to the business research process and to provide them with the skills to become information literate.

EVOLUTION OF AN UNDERGRADUATE BUSINESS INFORMATION CLASS

History of the Class

Starting in 1996 two sections of Information Retrieval for Business were offered to undergraduate business students as a one-credit pass/fail elective during the fall and spring semesters. Each section met twice a week for six weeks in a computer classroom. Due to limited seating in the computer classroom the enrollment for each section was capped at 30 students. The class proved popular with students and often had a wait list. In 2004, a third six-week section was added to meet the demand. Later in 2004, the business librarians applied for and were awarded an Innovations in Instructional Computing Award by the University of Iowa's Academic Technologies Advisory Council. The monetary award was used to hire a graduate assistant to help move the third section to online platforms (course management system and Elluminate). An online version of the class would accommodate a higher enrollment and also allow for flexibility in class scheduling.

The third section of the class debuted in the spring semester of 2006 as a synchronous online class through the platform Elluminate. In addition to the new format offering, the course was renamed Competitive Intelligence Resources to reflect the emphasis on competitive strategy in the business world. Later, in the fall of 2008, the third section moved to an asynchronous online environment. No longer limited to time and place, the new format enabled students to fit the one-credit class into their busy schedules.

The Class Today

Currently, the class is offered online asynchronously as one section with an enrollment of 55 students. There are no meeting times for the class, which is now called Searching for Business Information. Students view recordings and move through the course content in a six-week period. When creating the asynchronous class in the course management system, the instructors found it helpful to stick with the original weekly structure of the class: two lectures with corresponding research database demonstrations. However, rather than recording two long lectures, lectures are divided into parts and are under 20 minutes long. The recorded research databases demonstrations are very brief—under four minutes. Figure 23.1 shows one unit of the class as it appears in the course management system.

The topics covered in the class correspond with broad categories of business information: company information, industry and market information, business climate information, international business information, and article/book searching. During the first class the students are introduced not only to these categories, but also to information literacy.

The lecture highlights the ACRL (Association for College and Research Libraries) definition of information literacy and the skills required of an information-literate person. An information literate individual is able to

- Determine the extent of information needed
- Access the needed information effectively and efficiently
- Evaluate information and its sources critically
- Incorporate selected information into one's knowledge base
- Use information effectively to accomplish a specific purpose
- Understand the economic, legal, and social issues surrounding the use of information, and access and use information ethically and legally[3]

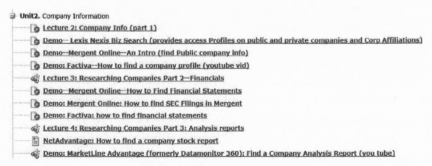

Figure 23.1.   Unit 2 of Searching for Business Information

When discussing the standards of information literacy in the first lecture, examples are used to demonstrate how the class will help them develop that skill. For example, when highlighting "Access the needed information effectively and efficiently," the instructor emphasizes that after students complete the class they will be able identify business sources that provide the information needed, such as financial information on a public company. After they have identified the appropriate source or sources, they will be able to retrieve the information quickly from that source. In my experience, students have the most questions and concerns about the last standard, in particular about citing sources. To help students understand why they should cite sources, the instructor asks them to think about citations as a map that will help other researchers see the source where they retrieved information and then explains that the researchers may go on to use that same source for their research purposes. In addition, the ACRL information literacy standards are echoed in the course objectives and learning outcomes, which are outlined in the class syllabus as shown in the appendix.

Throughout the six-week course, student information literacy and business research skills are assessed through the completion of four assignments and four multiple-choice quizzes. To pass the class students must complete all assignments satisfactorily and average a 60% on the quizzes.

In order to give the students a better understanding of why business research is conducted and how the information can be used, the assignments are scenario based. For example, the third assignment features the following scenario:

> You are interested in opening a sporting goods store in Des Moines, IA. To gain an understanding of the business environment/climate and to enable you to make better business decisions, you decide to search for demographic and economic statistics.

Then each question in the assignment builds on the main scenario. For example, one problem states,

> You would like to hire a retail sales staff. Search the Bureau of Labor and Statistics web site for the average wages of a retail salesperson and a retail sales manager in Iowa.

To help students further develop critical thinking skills, the quizzes also contain scenario-based questions. For example, one multiple-choice question asks,

> You are required to research a private company. What would be the best search strategy for finding information on a private company?
>
> a. Lexis Nexis Business Search, article databases, company website
> b. Marketresearch.com academic, article databases, company website
> c. EDGAR/SEC website, article databases, company website.

The scenarios on the assignments and the quizzes are topics that students may encounter in their other business class projects and also later in their business careers.

CONCLUSION

Undergraduate business students are required to complete a wide variety of research projects, such as company and industry research. Later, in their careers, they may also be called upon to conduct research on companies and industries. For almost 20 years, the for-credit business information class taught by librarians at the University of Iowa's Pomerantz Business Library has provided students with a strong foundation of information literacy skills. Through the class, librarians provide students with the business information research skills to succeed not only on the research projects that they may encounter in their business classes but also later in the workplace.

APPENDIX

Course Objectives and Expected Learning Outcomes

Objective 1: The successful student will leave the course with a deeper understanding of the unique nature of business information.

Specifically, each student will be able to

1. List three to five characteristics of business information
2. Explain how these characteristics impact the availability of information
3. Select an appropriate research strategy given the corresponding information landscape

Objective 2: Upon completion of this course, the successful student will be able to recognize the nature and extent of information needed for assignments common to most college level business courses.

Specifically, each student will be able to

1. Confer with instructors and participate in class discussions and peer work groups to identify a research topic
2. Identify key concepts and terms that describe the information needed

Objective 3: Students will be able to select the most appropriate resources to successfully complete assignments.

Specifically, each student will be able to

1. Identify the value and differences of potential resources in a variety of formats
2. Identify the purpose and audience of potential resources (e.g., popular versus trade versus scholarly)
3. Investigate the scope, content and organization of information resources
4. Formulate and describe criteria used to make information decisions and choices

Objective 4: Upon completion of this class, students will recognize the importance of critically analyzing information and will begin to do it themselves.

Specifically, each student will begin to

1. Evaluate information resources on a number of different criteria including but not limited to reliability, validity, accuracy, authority, timeliness, and point of view or bias

2. Recognize the importance of the context within which information is created
3. Establish his or her own criteria for determining validity of information

NOTES

1. Sokoloff, J. Information Literacy in the Workplace: Employer Expectations. *J Bus Fin Lib*. 2012;17(1): 1–17.
2. Ibid.
3. Association of College and Research Libraries. *Information Literacy Competency Standards for Higher Education*. 2000. http://www.acrl.org/ala/mgrps/divs/acrl/standards/standards.pdf. Accessed April 14, 2014.

24

The Expanding Role of Information Literacy in the Freshman Writing Program at Saint Louis University: A Case Study

Jamie L. Emery

BACKGROUND

Pius XII Memorial Library is the main library at Saint Louis University (SLU), a Catholic, Jesuit university in St. Louis, Missouri, with an enrollment of 12,222 undergraduate and graduate students as of fall 2012.[1] At SLU, students are required to take English 190: Advanced Strategies of Rhetoric and Research, the major composition course offered by the Department of English. Students in the SLU Parks College of Aviation, Engineering, and Technology may take an alternate course, English 192: Advanced Writing for Professionals. Both English 190 and 192 are research-intensive courses. Some students are also required to take a precursor to English 190/192, English 150: The Process of Composition, which requires only minimal research. Student placement in English 150 is determined by entering test scores. The vast majority of English 150 sections are taught as "stretch" courses, in which students and their instructors reunite the following semester for English 190, allowing for instructional continuity and scaffolding.

During the 2012–2013 academic year, roughly 1,520 SLU students enrolled in English 190 (76 sections, an estimated 20 students each). Approximately 80 students enrolled in the alternate course, English 192 (4 sections, 20 students each). About 320 students took English 150 (16 sections, 20 students each).

HISTORY

Research and instruction librarians at Pius XII Memorial Library have provided basic information literacy instruction to English 190/192 students for many years. Since 1988, librarians have paired with English 190/192 instructors and their courses to provide at least one classroom information literacy instruction session during the course of the semester. Librarians have also taught information literacy sessions for students in English 150 over the years, but more sporadically. Historically, information literacy instruction for English 150, 190, and 192 classes was virtually identical and students who took both English 150 and English 190 often complained about repetition. Research and instruction librarians faced difficulties trying to teach students basic information literacy skills during the course of only one or two class sessions.

Over the course of the 2007–2008 academic year, a library task force comprised of research and instruction librarians Martha Allen, Ron Crown, Jane Gillespie, John Montre, and Jamie Schmid (Emery) worked in consultation with Dr. Janice McIntire-Strasburg, writing program director, to develop an information literacy program that was mapped to the Freshman Writing Program curriculum. This program made the most of limited class time and prepared students at each course level to meet their particular information needs. The task force developed new learning outcomes for English 150 and English 190/192, two short video tutorials using Camtasia Studio (on finding books and finding articles), an online quantitative assessment using Easy Survey that was based upon the content in the tutorials, and an English 190/192 blog.

EXPANSION OF INFORMATION LITERACY PROGRAM

In the fall of 2008, research and instruction librarians introduced a stratified and blended information literacy program designed to empower SLU freshman to recognize their information needs and locate, evaluate, and use information effectively. Each section of each course (English 150, 190, and 192) was paired with a librarian who worked with the instructor and class for the semester. Students in English 150/190 stretch sections were paired with the same librarian for both English 150 and 190. All

English 192 courses, taken by SLU Parks College of Aviation, Engineering, and Technology students, were paired with the library's Parks College liaison librarian.

English 150: The Process of Composition instructors were required to bring their class to the library in person for one 50- or 75-minute instruction session in which the class librarian gave students a brief introduction to finding materials in the library. Students then worked in pairs using the library catalog and a location guide to find a list of specific items in the library, locate them on the shelf, and bring them back to the classroom. When students returned to the classroom with their items, the librarian talked with them about their experiences and any challenges they faced. This self-led tour was designed to help English 150 students feel more comfortable in the library and prepare them for more advanced English 190 information literacy instruction the next semester.

English 190: Advanced Strategies of Rhetoric and Research and English 192: Advanced Writing for Professionals instructors were required to assign the viewing of two Camtasia video tutorials ("Finding Books in the SLU Libraries" and "Finding Articles on a Topic") as well as the completion of an online library assessment based upon tutorial content. The quantitative, online assessment was used to assess basic information literacy competencies and track tutorial participation. It consisted of 13 multiple-choice questions designed to measure specific library skills. Instructors were required to have their students watch the tutorials and complete the online assessment during the first four weeks of the semester. The class librarian reviewed the assessment results and shared them with the course instructor before the class visited the library for in-person instruction. Instructors were required to bring their classes to the library for at least one 75-minute or two 50-minute class periods. During these in-person instruction sessions, the class librarian built upon tutorial and assessment content and focused on more sophisticated library research skills such as advanced search strategies and information evaluation. At the end of the last in-person instruction session, students completed a qualitative one-minute paper assessment that encouraged them to ask questions about concepts that were still unclear to them. The librarian responded to these questions after class via the English 190/192 blog, then shared their post with the instructor, who in turn shared it with his or her class.

Students in English 150, 190, and 192 were encouraged to ask their librarian questions outside of class and take advantage of one-on-one, personalized research consultations. Additional resources for students included a Freshman Writing Program research guide, a virtual library tour, Ask a Librarian services, and plagiarism prevention resources.

PROGRAM EVALUATION

In 2011, the library task force held instructor focus groups and conducted an online survey to assess the effectiveness of freshman writing information literacy instruction. Based on information collected as well as assessment results and librarian feedback, the task force gradually made the following changes to the program.

All English 190/192 instructors are now required bring their class to the library for at least two in-person information literacy instruction sessions. Librarians also offer a walk-in Library Lab service for students in English 150, 190, and 192. The Library Lab is open four hours per week and staffed by research and instruction librarians, who provide research consultations to students without an appointment. Some instructors offer their students extra credit for attending Library Lab or meeting with their class librarian for research consultations. Technological changes have prompted moving the English 190/192 online library assessment to Qualtrix, the English 190/192 blog question and answer pairs to LibAnswers, and the Freshman Writing Program research guide to LibGuides. Links to these resources are available at http://libraries.slu.edu/resources/fwplc.

KEYS TO OUR SUCCESS

Looking back on the expansion of the freshman writing information literacy program, librarians at Pius XII Memorial Library view the following as important keys to our success.

- Librarians at Pius XII Memorial Library have had a strong relationship with the English Department Writing Program for many years. We didn't have to get our foot in the door with the program; we only needed to gradually widen it. The collaboration and support of the Writing Program director, Dr. Janice McIntire-Strasburg, has been essential.

- Information literacy content is mapped to the curriculum. Material covered is relevant to students and their courses, and they're able to apply what they learn immediately.
- Information literacy content is stratified. Students in English 150 and English 190/192 are now taught different, course-relevant skills.
- We make the most of limited class time with students by bringing portions of information literacy instruction outside of the classroom using tutorials, online assessment, and research consultations.
- The program is truly a team effort as all twelve research and instruction librarians at Pius XII Memorial Library participate.
- Pairing English 150/190 stretch courses with the same librarian for two back-to-back semesters ensures continuity and allows for relationship building.
- Our program is based upon shared learning outcomes, but leaves librarians free to teach the agreed-upon content as they see fit. It is structured, but still flexible.
- Changes to the program are very gradual as we develop and refine it over time.
- The program is easily modified. We're able to adapt to changes in technology, curriculum, and student baseline knowledge and improve the program. As freshman writing courses change, we change with them.
- Freshman writing courses themselves are very structured and all instructors use the same basic syllabus. Most of the instructors are graduate students and do not expect the same level of pedagogical autonomy as full-time faculty. This increases instructor buy-in and participation in the program.
- As coordinator of the freshman writing information literacy program, I'm in regular contact with the Writing Program director and instructors. I meet with instructors at their orientation each semester, provide a program overview, remind instructors about their program-related responsibilities, and address questions and concerns.

CHALLENGES

No information literacy program is perfect, and librarians at Pius XII Memorial Library face the following challenges:

- Classroom time with students is still limited.
- While online tutorials and assessment help address the issue of limited classroom time, they require regular, time-consuming updates.
- The reliability and responsiveness of instructors varies, at times making scheduling in-person sessions a challenge.
- Librarians are not always involved in freshman writing curricular changes. As a result, we must sometimes adjust the information literacy program on the fly.

CONCLUSION

The gradual expansion of information literacy in the Freshman Writing Program allowed us to advance our own initiatives while supporting the needs of the program. This process has taken several years, but our partnership has led to a natural progression in curriculum integration. We are currently collaborating with teaching faculty on revisions to the English 190 syllabus and research assignments. It is our hope that the role of information literacy and librarians in the Freshman Writing Program will continue to evolve to meet the educational needs of SLU students.

APPENDIX

Library Instruction Outcomes for English 150, 190, and 192

Research Librarians at Pius XII Memorial Library offer online video tutorials and in-person library instruction sessions and tours for English 150, English 190, and English 192 classes. Each class is partnered with a librarian who will teach the instruction session(s) and is available by appointment for individual consultations to provide more in-depth research assistance.

Library Instruction Outcomes for English 150

The English 150 student will

- Identify available library resources and services (e.g. Ask a Librarian) in order to utilize them to meet information needs

- Recognize that information in libraries is organized by subject in order to facilitate access
- Recognize the existence of classification schemes and other systems (e.g. call number systems, catalogs, or databases) in order to locate library resources

Library Instruction Outcomes for English 190 and English 192

The English 190 or English 192 student will

- Distinguish between library catalogs, general and specialized databases, and web search engines in order to select the most appropriate resource for research
- Search library catalogs, databases, and the Web using flexible vocabulary and Boolean logic in order to retrieve sources that are topic relevant
- Utilize Library of Congress subject headings in library catalogs and subject descriptors in databases in order to locate related and relevant sources
- Examine and compare information from various sources in order to evaluate reliability, validity, accuracy, authority, timeliness, and point of view or bias
- Interpret bibliographic citations in order to facilitate access to information and reinforce accurate source citation
- Recognize the importance of acknowledging the use of information sources in order to avoid plagiarism.

NOTES

1. Saint Louis University Office of Institutional Research. *Fact Book, 2012–2013.* St. Louis, MO: Saint Louis University Office of Institutional Research; 2013. http://www.slu.edu/Documents/provost/oir/Fact%20Book%20 2012-2013%20FINAL.pdf. Accessed December 9, 2013.

Index

active learning, 41, 44, 46–51, 62,
75–76, 85, 96, 98, 105–6, 155, 175,
181
ADDIE, 4–5
adult learning, 27–28, 38–42
andragogy. *See* adult learning
assessment, 58–59, 62, 66–67, 88,
91, 98–99, 109–10, 116, 144, 151,
155–56; examples of assessment,
162, 168–70, 181, 191, 197, 208–9,
221; Group Readiness Assessment
Test, 78–79; Individual Readiness
Assessment Test, 78; peer
evaluation, team based learning,
81; peer evaluation of instruction,
59, 110, 127–31; self-evaluation,
124–27
audience response systems, 4, 7, 50,
109

behaviorism, 27, 45
Blackboard. *See* course management
systems
blended learning, 49, 95, 113–14,
120–21

Bloom's Taxonomy. *See* learning
objectives
clickers. *See* audience response
systems
cognitive science research, 46
collaboration with teaching faculty, 8,
12, 15, 100, 113, 158–59, 179, 195,
199–200, 207
constructivism, 45–46
course management systems, 6,
15, 95–96, 98, 118, 155, 161,
167
curriculum committees, 9, 11–12, 20,
159, 162, 196
curriculum-based instruction, 11,
108–9, 149, 156, 166, 172, 175

Desire2Learn. *See* course management
systems
Dewey, John, 25–26, 39
distance learning, 15, 38, 41, 95–96,
100, 113, 167, 195
Dunn and Dunn Learning Style
Model. *See* learning styles

embedded librarians, 7, 15, 20, 100–101, 195
evaluation. *See* assessment
evidence-based practice, 8, 11, 41, 63, 77, 87–88, 99, 139–42, 149, 150–51, 159, 171

face-to-face, 75, 77
Fleming, Neil. *See* VARK model
flipped classrooms, 49, 116–17, 175

Gardner, Howard, 26–27

information literacy, 3, 11–13, 35, 40, 63, 67, 87–88, 150, 189, 214, 219
instruction materials, 59–60, 97
instructional design, 4–6, 41, 105–6, 119

Knowles, Malcolm, 27, 39–41
Kolb Experiential Learning Theory. *See* learning styles

learning objectives, 5, 31, 41, 48, 56, 66, 105, 150, 215–16, 223–24; Bloom's Taxonomy, 31–33, 56, 66
learning styles, 28–31, 106, 114–15, 125; Dunn and Dunn Learning Style Model, 28–30; Kolb Experiential Learning Theory, 29–30; VARK model, 29–30
liaisons, 7–9, 14, 206
library events, 17, 20, 208
lifelong learners, 38, 41

Moodle. *See* course management systems

nontraditional students. *See* returning students

online instruction, 58, 95
open house. *See* library events
outreach, 8, 166

peer evaluation. *See* assessment
perform. *See* presentation skills
Piaget, 26
PICO, 31, 141, 159, 167
presentation skills, 57, 107
problem-based learning, 41, 44, 46–47, 49–50, 109, 172
PubMed, 6, 78, 81–82, 99, 141, 146, 159–61, 171

quizzes, 101, 214

relationship building, 14, 16, 56, 149, 155, 173–74
returning students, 37–38, 41

Skinner, B. F. *See* behaviorism
statistics, 101, 162, 214

team-based learning, 44, 109, 145
team-teaching, 130, 174, 195–96
technology, 40, 65, 96, 106, 109, 112, 119, 177
traditional students, 35–37
tutorials, 14, 38, 78, 83, 96–101, 109, 112, 143, 146, 155, 159–62, 167, 201, 219–20, 222–23

VARK model. *See* learning styles

About the Editors

Amy E. Blevins, MALS, holds the rank of expert librarian at the Hardin Library for the Health Sciences at the University of Iowa. She serves as a clinical education librarian and is the liaison to the Carver College of Medicine as well as a liaison to several departments within the University of Iowa Hospitals and Clinics. She previously worked as the education and instructional technologies librarian at the William E. Laupus Health Sciences Library at East Carolina University. In addition to holding a MALS, Amy also has a certificate in distance learning and administration from East Carolina University.

Megan B. Inman, MLIS, holds the rank of research assistant professor at the William E. Laupus Health Sciences Library at East Carolina University. She serves as the liaison to the College of Allied Health Sciences and the College of Health and Human Performance. As a liaison, Megan works closely with faculty to incorporate library instruction into their curriculum. She embedded in multiple online courses that provide users with library materials and instruction at their point of need.

List of Contributors

Christine Andresen, MLS
Instructional Design Librarian
Laupus Health Sciences Library
East Carolina University
andresenc@ecu.edu

Adam T. Beauchamp, MLIS
Research and Instruction Librarian (Social Sciences)
Howard-Tilton Memorial Library
Tulane University
abeaucha@tulane.edu

Kimberly Bloedel, MA
Head
Pomerantz Business Library
University of Iowa
Kimberly-bloedel@uiowa.edu

Sarah Cantrell, MALIS
Clinical Librarian
Darnall Medical Library
Walter Reed National Military Medical Center
sarah.cantrell@gmail.com

Allison Carr, MLIS
Librarian
CSUSM Library
California State University at San Marcos
acarr@csusm.edu

Jessica Cole, MLIS, AHIP
Academic Programs Librarian
Phoenix Biomedical Campus Library
Northern Arizona University
jessica.cole@nau.edu

April Cunningham, MLIS, EdD
Instruction/Information Literacy Librarian
Palomar College Library
Palomar College
acunningham@palomar.edu

Jennifer Deberg, OT(BS), MLS
Clinical Education Librarian
Hardin Library for the Health Sciences
University of Iowa
Jennifer-deberg@uiowa.edu

Jamie L. Emery, MS
Research and Instruction Librarian
Associate Professor
Pius XII Memorial Library
Saint Louis University
jemery2@slu.edu

Daniel Gall, MLIS
Coordinator of Library Services for Distance Education
Liaison Librarian for Social Work
University of Iowa Libraries
University of Iowa
daniel-gall@uiowa.edu

Rebecca S. Graves, MLS
Educational Services Librarian
J. Otto Lottes Health Sciences Library
University of Missouri
GravesR@health.missouri.edu

Barbara A. Gushrowski, MLS, AHIP
Manager of Library Services
Community Health Network
BGushrowski@ecommunity.com

Eric Jennings, MA
Instruction and Outreach Librarian
McIntyre Library
University of Wisconsin–Eau Claire
jenninge@uwec.edu

Emily M. Johnson, MLIS
Regional Assistant Librarian and Assistant Professor
Library of the Health Sciences–Peoria
University of Illinois at Chicago
emj11@uic.edu

Rienne Johnson, MLIS
Assistant Professor of Pharmacy Practice
Reference Librarian
Oliver Ocasek Regional Medical Information Center
Northeast Ohio Medical University
rjohnson1@neomed.edu

Hans Kishel, MS, MS
Research and Instruction Librarian
McIntyre Library
University of Wisconsin–Eau Claire
kishelhf@uwec.edu

Susan Kraat, MLS
Associate Librarian (retired)
Coordinator of Instructional Services, 2002–2013,
Sojourner Truth Library
State University of New York at New Paltz

Adrianne Leonardelli, MLIS
Research and Education Librarian
Liaison to School of Nursing
Medical Center Library and Archives
Duke University
adrianne.leonardelli@duke.edu

Stephan J. Macaluso, MM, MLS
Coordinator of Distance Learning Library Services
Sojourner Truth Library
State University of New York at New Paltz
macaluss@newpaltz.edu

Mark P. MacEachern, MLIS
Informationist
Taubman Health Sciences Library
University of Michigan
markmac@umich.edu

Michele Malloy, MALIS
Research Services Coordinator
Dahlgren Memorial Library
Georgetown University Medical Center
mlm236@georgetown.edu

Shelly R. McDavid, MEd, MLS
Library Information Assistant
Zalk Veterinary Medical Library
University of Missouri
mcdavids@missouri.edu

Heather A. McEwen, MLIS, MS
Curriculum Mapper for the College of Medicine
Instructor of Family and Community Medicine
Assistant Professor of Pharmacy Practice
Northeast Ohio Medical University
hm2@neomed.edu

Connie Schardt, MLS, AHIP, FMLA
Adjunct Faculty
School of Information and Library Science
University of North Carolina at Chapel Hill
schardt@unc.edu

Carolyn Schubert, MLIS
Health Sciences and Nursing Librarian
Rose Library
James Madison University
Schubecf@jmu.edu

Janice M. Spalding, MD
Vice Chair and Associate Professor
Department of Family and Community Medicine
Northeast Ohio Medical University
jmspaldi@neomed.edu

David M. Sperling, MD
Clinical Curriculum Director
Northeast Ohio Medical University
sperlind@summahealth.org

LuAnne M. Stockton, BA, BS
Curriculum Coordinator and Instructor of Family and Community
    Medicine
Northeast Ohio Medical University
LSTOCKTO@neomed.edu

Whitney Townsend, MLIS
Informationist
Taubman Health Sciences Library
University of Michigan
Whiteyt@umich.edu

Brandi Tuttle, MSLIS, AHIP
Research and Education Librarian
Liaison to Physician Assistant Program
Medical Center Library and Archives
Duke University
brandi.tuttle@duke.edu

Bryan S. Vogh, MA
Assistant Professor
Head, Library Systems
McIntyre Library
University of Wisconsin–Eau Claire
voghbs@uwec.edu

Katy Kavanagh Webb, MA, MILS
Instructional Design Librarian
Joyner Library
East Carolina University
kavanaghk@ecu.edu

Lisa N. Weiss, MD, MEd
Associate Dean of Curriculum
College of Medicine
Northeast Ohio Medical University
lisanweiss@gmail.com